# Parleyings by Robert Browning

**WITH CERTAIN PEOPLE OF IMPORTANCE IN THEIR DAY**

Robert Browning is one of the most significant Victorian Poets and, of course, English Poetry.

Much of his reputation is based upon his mastery of the dramatic monologue although his talents encompassed verse plays and even a well-regarded essay on Shelley during a long and prolific career.

He was born on May 7th, 1812 in Walmouth, London. Much of his education was home based and Browning was an eclectic and studious student, learning several languages and much else across a myriad of subjects, interests and passions.

Browning's early career began promisingly. The fragment from his intended long poem Pauline brought him to the attention of Dante Gabriel Rossetti, and was followed by Paracelsus, which was praised by both William Wordsworth and Charles Dickens. In 1840 the difficult Sordello, which was seen as willfully obscure, brought his career almost to a standstill.

Despite these artistic and professional difficulties his personal life was about to become immensely fulfilling. He began a relationship with, and then married, the older and better known Elizabeth Barrett. This new foundation served to energise his writings, his life and his career.

During their time in Italy they both wrote much of their best work. With her untimely death in 1861 he returned to London and thereafter began several further major projects.

The collection Dramatis Personae (1864) and the book-length epic poem The Ring and the Book (1868-69) were published and well received; his reputation as a venerated English poet now assured.

Robert Browning died in Venice on December 12th, 1889.

## Index of Contents

*IN MEMORIAM J. MILSAND, OBIIT IV. SEPTEMBER, MDCCCLXXXVI.*

*Absens Absentem Auditque Videtque.*

## APOLLO AND THE FATES

## A PROLOGUE

*(Hymn in Mercurium, v. 559. Eumenides, vv. 693-4, 697-8. Alcestis, vv. 12, 33.)*

**APOLLO** [From above]
Flame at my footfall, Parnassus! Apollo,
Breaking ablaze on thy topmost peak,
Burns thence, down to the depths—dread hollow—
Haunt of the Dire Ones. Haste! They wreak
Wrath on Admetus whose respite I seek.


**THE FATES** [Below. Darkness]
Dragonwise couched in the womb of our Mother,
Coiled at thy nourishing heart's core, Night!
Dominant Dreads, we, one by the other,
Deal to each mortal his dole of light
On earth—the upper, the glad, the bright.

**CLOTHO**
Even so: thus from my loaded spindle
Plucking a pinch of the fleece, lo, "Birth"
Brays from my bronze lip: life I kindle:
Look, 't is a man! go, measure on earth
The minute thy portion, whatever its worth!

\*   \*   \*   \*   \*


**LACHESIS**
Woe-purfled, weal-prankt,—if it speed, if it linger,—
Life's substance and show are determined by me,
Who, meting out, mixing with sure thumb and finger,
Lead life the due length: is all smoothness and glee,
All tangle and grief? Take the lot, my decree!

\*   \*   \*   \*   \*

**ATROPOS**

—Which I make an end of: the smooth as the tangled
My shears cut asunder: each snap shrieks "One more
Mortal makes sport for us Moirai who dangled
The puppet grotesquely till earth's solid floor
Proved film he fell through, lost in Naught as before."

\*     \*     \*     \*     \*

**CLOTHO**
I spin thee a thread. Live, Admetus! Produce him!

**LACHESIS**
Go,—brave, wise, good, happy! Now chequer the thread!
He is slaved for, yet loved by a god. I unloose him
A goddess-sent plague. He has conquered, is wed,
Men crown him, he stands at the height,—

**ATROPOS**
He is ...

**APOLLO** [Entering: Light]
"Dead?"

Nay, swart spinsters! So I surprise you
Making and marring the fortunes of Man?
Huddling—no marvel, your enemy eyes you—
Head by head bat-like, blots under the ban
Of daylight earth's blessing since time began!

\*     \*     \*     \*     \*

**THE FATES**
Back to thy blest earth, prying Apollo!
Shaft upon shaft transpierce with thy beams
Earth to the centre,—spare but this hollow
Hewn out of Night's heart, where our mystery seems
Mewed from day's malice: wake earth from her dreams!

\*     \*     \*     \*     \*

**APOLLO**
Crones, 't is your dusk selves I startle from slumber:
Day's god deposes you—queens Night-crowned!
—Plying your trade in a world ye encumber,
Fashioning Man's web of life—spun, wound,
Left the length ye allot till a clip strews the ground!

Behold I bid truce to your doleful amusement—

Annulled by a sunbeam!

**THE FATES**
Boy, are not we peers?

**APOLLO**
You with the spindle grant birth: whose inducement
But yours—with the niggardly digits—endears
To mankind chance and change, good and evil? Your shears ...

\*     \*     \*     \*     \*

**ATROPOS**
Ay, mine end the conflict: so much is no fable.
We spin, draw to length, cut asunder: what then?
So it was, and so is, and so shall be: art able
To alter life's law for ephemeral men?

**APOLLO**
Nor able nor willing. To threescore and ten

Extend but the years of Admetus! Disaster
O'ertook me, and, banished by Zeus, I became
A servant to one who forbore me though master:
True lovers were we.  Discontinue your game,
Let him live whom I loved, then hate on, all the same!

\*     \*     \*     \*     \*

**THE FATES**
And what if we granted—law-flouter, use-trampler—
His life at the suit of an upstart? Judge, thou—
Of joy were it fuller, of span because ampler?
For love's sake, not hate's, end Admetus—ay, now—
Not a gray hair on head, nor a wrinkle on brow!

For, boy, 't is illusion: from thee comes a glimmer
Transforming to beauty life blank at the best.
Withdraw—and how looks life at worst, when to shimmer
Succeeds the sure shade, and Man's lot frowns—confessed
Mere blackness chance-brightened?  Whereof shall attest

The truth this same mortal, the darling thou stylest,
Whom love would advantage,—eke out, day by day,
A life which 't is solely thyself reconcilest
Thy friend to endure,—life with hope: take away
Hope's gleam from Admetus, he spurns it. For, say—

What 's infancy? Ignorance, idleness, mischief:
Youth ripens to arrogance, foolishness, greed:
Age—impotence, churlishness, rancor: call this chief
Of boons for thy loved one? Much rather bid speed
Our function, let live whom thou hatest indeed!

Persuade thee, bright boy-thing!  Our eld be instructive!

**APOLLO**
And certes youth owns the experience of age.
Ye hold then, grave seniors, my beams are productive
—They solely—of good that 's mere semblance, engage
Man's eye—gilding evil, Man's true heritage?

\*    \*    \*    \*    \*

**THE FATES**
So, even so! From without,—at due distance
If viewed,—set a-sparkle, reflecting thy rays,—
Life mimics the sun: but withdraw such assistance,
The counterfeit goes, the reality stays—
An ice-ball disguised as a fire-orb.

**APOLLO**
What craze

Possesses the fool then whose fancy conceits him
As happy?

**THE FATES**
Man happy?

**APOLLO**
If otherwise—solve
This doubt which besets me! What friend ever greets him
Except with "Live long as the seasons revolve,"
Not "Death to thee straightway"? Your doctrines absolve

Such hailing from hatred: yet Man should know best.
He talks it, and glibly, as life were a load
Man fain would be rid of: when put to the test,
He whines "Let it lie, leave me trudging the road
That is rugged so far, but methinks" ...

**THE FATES**
Ay, 't is owed

To that glamour of thine, he bethinks him "Once past

The stony, some patch, nay, a smoothness of swarth
Awaits my tired foot: life turns easy at last"—
Thy largess so lures him, he looks for reward
Of the labor and sorrow.

**APOLLO**
It seems, then—debarred

Of illusion—(I needs must acknowledge the plea)
Man desponds and despairs. Yet,—still further to draw
Due profit from counsel,—suppose there should be
Some power in himself, some compensative law
By virtue of which, independently ...

\*     \*     \*     \*     \*

**THE FATES**
Faugh!
Strength hid in the weakling!
What bowl-shape hast there,
Thus laughingly proffered? A gift to our shrine?
Thanks—worsted in argument! Not so? Declare
Its purpose!

**APOLLO**
I proffer earth's product, not mine.
Taste, try, and approve Man's invention of—WINE!

\*     \*     \*     \*     \*

**THE FATES**
We feeding suck honeycombs.

**APOLLO**
Sustenance meagre!
Such fare breeds the fumes that show all things amiss.
Quaff wine,—how the spirits rise nimble and eager,
Unscale the dim eyes! To Man's cup grant one kiss
Of your lip, then allow—no enchantment like this!

\*     \*     \*     \*     \*

**CLOTHO**
Unhook wings, unhood brows! Dost hearken?

**LACHESIS**
I listen:
I see—smell the food these fond mortals prefer

To our feast, the bee's bounty!

**ATROPOS**
The thing leaps! But—glisten
Its best, I withstand it—unless all concur
In adventure so novel.

**APOLLO**
Ye drink?

**THE FATES**
We demur.

*     *     *     *     *

**APOLLO**
Sweet Trine, be indulgent nor scout the contrivance
Of Man—Bacchus-prompted! The juice, I uphold,
Illuminates gloom without sunny connivance,
Turns fear into hope and makes cowardice bold,—
Touching all that is leadlike in life turns it gold!

*     *     *     *     *

**THE FATES**
Faith foolish as false!

**APOLLO**
But essay it, soft sisters!
Then mock as ye may. Lift the chalice to lip!
Good: thou next—and thou! Seems the web, to you twisters
Of life's yarn, so worthless?

**CLOTHO**
Who guessed that one sip
Would impart such a lightness of limb?

**LACHESIS**
I could skip

In a trice from the pied to the plain in my woof!
What parts each from either? A hair's breadth, no inch.
Once learn the right method of stepping aloof,
Though on black next foot falls, firm I fix it, nor flinch,
—Such my trust white succeeds!

**ATROPOS**
One could live—at a pinch!

**APOLLO**

What, beldames? Earth's yield, by Man's skill, can effect
Such a cure of sick sense that ye spy the relation
Of evil to good? But drink deeper, correct
Blear sight more convincingly still! Take your station
Beside me, drain dregs! Now for edification!

Whose gift have ye gulped? Thank not me but my brother,
Blithe Bacchus, our youngest of godships. 'T was he
Found all boons to all men, by one god or other
Already conceded, so judged there must be
New guerdon to grace the new advent, you see!

Else how would a claim to Man's homage arise?
The plan lay arranged of his mixed woe and weal,
So disposed—such Zeus' will—with design to make wise
The witless—that false things were mingled with real,
Good with bad: such the lot whereto law set the seal.

Now, human of instinct—since Semele's son,
Yet minded divinely—since fathered by Zeus,
With naught Bacchus tampered, undid not things done,
Owned wisdom anterior, would spare wont and use,
Yet change—without shock to old rule—introduce.

Regard how your cavern from crag-tip to base
Frowns sheer, height and depth adamantine, one death!
I rouse with a beam the whole rampart, displace
No splinter—yet see how my flambeau, beneath
And above, bids this gem wink, that crystal unsheathe!

Withdraw beam—disclosure once more Night forbids you
Of spangle and sparkle—Day's chance-gift, surmised
Rock's permanent birthright: my potency rids you
No longer of darkness, yet light—recognized—
Proves darkness a mask: day lives on though disguised.

If Bacchus by wine's aid avail so to fluster
Your sense, that life's fact grows from adverse and thwart
To helpful and kindly by means of a cluster—
Mere hand-squeeze, earth's nature sublimed by Man's art—
Shall Bacchus claim thanks wherein Zeus has no part?

Zeus—wisdom anterior? No, maids, be admonished!
If morn's touch at base worked such wonders, much more

Had noontide in absolute glory astonished
Your den, filled a-top to o'erflowing. I pour
No such mad confusion. 'T is Man's to explore

Up and down, inch by inch, with the taper his reason:
No torch, it suffices—held deftly and straight.
Eyes, purblind at first, feel their way in due season,
Accept good with bad, till unseemly debate
Turns concord—despair, acquiescence in fate.

Who works this but Zeus? Are not instinct and impulse,
Not concept and incept his work through Man's soul
On Man's sense? Just as wine ere it reach brain must brim pulse,
Zeus' flash stings the mind that speeds body to goal,
Bids pause at no part but press on, reach the whole.

For petty and poor is the part ye envisage
When—(quaff away, cummers!)—ye view, last and first,
As evil Man's earthly existence. Come! Is age,
Is infancy—manhood—so uninterspersed
With good—some faint sprinkle?

**CLOTHO**
I 'd speak if I durst.

\*     \*     \*     \*     \*

**APOLLO**
Draughts dregward loose tongue-tie.

**LACHESIS**
I 'd see, did no web
Set eyes somehow winking.

**APOLLO**
Drains-deep lies their purge
—True collyrium!

**ATROPOS**
Words, surging at high-tide, soon ebb
From starved ears.

**APOLLO**
Drink but down to the source, they resurge.
Join hands! Yours and yours too! A dance or a dirge?

\*     \*     \*     \*     \*

**CLOTHO**

Quashed be our quarrel! Sourly and smilingly,
Bare and gowned, bleached limbs and browned,
Drive we a dance, three and one, reconcilingly,
Thanks to the cup where dissension is drowned,
Defeat proves triumphant and slavery crowned.

Infancy? What if the rose-streak of morning
Pale and depart in a passion of tears?
Once to have hoped is no matter for scorning!
Love once—e'en love's disappointment endears!
A minute's success pays the failure of years.

Manhood—the actual? Nay, praise the potential!
(Bound upon bound, foot it around!)
What is? No, what may be—sing! that 's Man's essential!
(Ramp, tramp, stamp and compound
Fancy with fact—the lost secret is found!)

Age? Why, fear ends there: the contest concluded,
Man did live his life, did escape from the fray:
Not scratchless but unscathed, he somehow eluded
Each blow fortune dealt him, and conquers to-day:
To-morrow—new chance and fresh strength,—might we say?

Laud then Man's life—no defeat but a triumph!

[Explosion from the earth's centre.

**CLOTHO**

Ha, loose hands!

**LACHESIS**

I reel in a swound.

**ATROPOS**

Horror yawns under me, while from on high—humph!
Lightnings astound, thunders resound,
Vault-roof reverberates, groans the ground!

[Silence.

**APOLLO**

I acknowledge.

**THE FATES**

Hence, trickster! Straight sobered are we!
The portent assures 't was our tongue spoke the truth,

Not thine. While the vapor encompassed us three
We conceived and bore knowledge—a bantling uncouth,
Old brains shudder back from: so—take it, rash youth!

Lick the lump into shape till a cry comes!

**APOLLO**
I hear.

**THE FATES**
Dumb music, dead eloquence! Say it, or sing!
What was quickened in us and thee also?

**APOLLO**
I fear.

**THE FATES**
Half female, half male—go, ambiguous thing!
While we speak—perchance sputter—pick up what we fling!

Known yet ignored, nor divined nor unguessed,
Such is Man's law of life. Do we strive to declare
What is ill, what is good in our spinning? Worst, best,
Change hues of a sudden: now here and now there
Flits the sign which decides: all about yet nowhere.

'T is willed so,—that Man's life be lived, first to last,
Up and down, through and through—not in portions, forsooth,
To pick and to choose from. Our shuttles fly fast,
Weave living, not life sole and whole: as age—youth,
So death completes living, shows life in its truth.

Man learningly lives: till death helps him—no lore!
It is doom and must be. Dost submit?

**APOLLO**
I assent—
Concede but Admetus! So much if no more
Of my prayer grant as peace-pledge! Be gracious, though, blent,
Good and ill, love and hate streak your life-gift!

**THE FATES**
Content!

Such boon we accord in due measure. Life's term
We lengthen should any be moved for love's sake
To forego life's fulfilment, renounce in the germ
Fruit mature—bliss or woe—either infinite. Take

Or leave thy friend's lot: on his head be the stake!

\*    \*    \*    \*    \*

**APOLLO**
On mine, griesly gammers! Admetus, I know thee!
Thou prizest the right these unwittingly give
Thy subjects to rush, pay obedience they owe thee!
Importunate one with another they strive
For the glory to die that their king may survive.

Friends rush: and who first in all Pheræ appears
But thy father to serve as thy substitute?

**CLOTHO**
Bah!

**APOLLO**
Ye wince? Then his mother, well stricken in years,
Advances her claim—or his wife—

**LACHESIS**
Tra-la-la!

**APOLLO**
But he spurns the exchange, rather dies!

**ATROPOS**
Ha, ha, ha!

[**APOLLO** ascends. Darkness.


WITH BERNARD DE MANDEVILLE

I

Ay, this same midnight, by this chair of mine,
Come and review thy counsels: art thou still
Stanch to their teaching?—not as fools opine
Its purport might be, but as subtler skill
Could, through turbidity, the loaded line
Of logic casting, sound deep, deeper, till
It touched a quietude and reached a shrine
And recognized harmoniously combine
Evil with good, and hailed truth's triumph.—thine,
Sage dead long since, Bernard de Mandeville!

II

Only, 't is no fresh knowledge that I crave,
Fuller truth yet, new gainings from the grave;
Here we alive must needs deal fairly, turn
To what account Man may Man's portion, learn
Man's proper play with truth in part, before
Entrusted with the whole. I ask no more
Than smiling witness that I do my best
With doubtful doctrine: afterwards the rest!
So, silent face me while I think and speak!
A full disclosure? Such would outrage law.
Law deals the same with soul and body: seek
Full truth my soul may, when some babe, I saw
A new-born weakling, starts up strong—not weak—
Man every whit, absolved from earning awe,
Pride, rapture, if the soul attains to wreak
Its will on flesh, at last can thrust, lift, draw,
As mind bids muscle—mind which long has striven,
Painfully urging body's impotence
To effort whereby—once law's barrier riven,
Life's rule abolished—body might dispense
With infancy's probation, straight be given
—Not by foiled darings, fond attempts back-driven,
Fine faults of growth, brave sins which saint when shriven—
To stand full-statured in magnificence.


III

No: as with body so deals law with soul
That 's stung to strength through weakness, strives for good
Through evil,—earth its race-ground, heaven its goal,
Presumably: so far I understood
Thy teaching long ago. But what means this
—Objected by a mouth which yesterday
Was magisterial in antithesis
To half the truths we hold, or trust we may,
Though tremblingly the while? "No sign"—groaned he—
"No stirring of God's finger to denote
He wills that right should have supremacy
On earth, not wrong! How helpful could we quote
But one poor instance when he interposed
Promptly and surely and beyond mistake
Between oppression and its victim, closed
Accounts with sin for once, and bade us wake

From our long dream that justice bears no sword,
Or else forgets whereto its sharpness serves!
So might we safely mock at what unnerves
Faith now, be spared the sapping fear's increase
That haply evil's strife with good shall cease
Never on earth. Nay, after earth, comes peace
Born out of life-long battle? Man's lip curves
With scorn: there, also, what if justice swerves
From dealing doom, sets free by no swift stroke
Right fettered here by wrong, but leaves life's yoke—
Death should loose man from—fresh laid, past release?"


IV


Bernard de Mandeville, confute for me
This parlous friend who captured or set free
Thunderbolts at his pleasure, yet would draw
Back, panic-stricken by some puny straw
Thy gold-rimmed amber-headed cane had whisked
Out of his pathway if the object risked
Encounter, 'scaped thy kick from buckled shoe!
As when folk heard thee in old days pooh-pooh
Addison's tye-wig preachment, grant this friend—
(Whose groan I hear, with guffaw at the end
Disposing of mock-melancholy)—grant
His bilious mood one potion, ministrant
Of homely wisdom, healthy wit! For, hear!
"With power and will, let preference appear
By intervention ever and aye, help good
When evil's mastery is understood
In some plain outrage, and triumphant wrong
Tramples weak right to nothingness: nay, long
Ere such sad consummation brings despair
To right's adherents, ah, what help it were
If wrong lay strangled in the birth—each head
Of the hatched monster promptly crushed, instead
Of spared to gather venom! We require
No great experience that the inch-long worm,
Free of our heel, would grow to vomit fire,
And one day plague the world in dragon form.
So should wrong merely peep abroad to meet
Wrong's due quietus, leave our world's way safe
For honest walking."


V

Sage, once more repeat
Instruction! 'T is a sore to soothe not chafe.
Ah, Fabulist, what luck, could I contrive
To coax from thee another "Grumbling Hive"!
My friend himself wrote fables short and sweet:
Ask him—"Suppose the Gardener of Man's ground
Plants for a purpose, side by side with good,
Evil—(and that he does so—look around!
What does the field show?)—were it understood
That purposely the noxious plant was found
Vexing the virtuous, poison close to food,
If, at first stealing-forth of life in stalk
And leaflet-promise, quick his spud should balk
Evil from budding foliage, bearing fruit?
Such timely treatment of the offending root
Might strike the simple as wise husbandry,
But swift sure extirpation would scarce suit
Shrewder observers. Seed once sown thrives: why
Frustrate its product, miss the quality
Which sower binds himself to count upon?
Had seed fulfilled the destined purpose, gone
Unhindered up to harvest—what know I
But proof were gained that every growth of good
Sprang consequent on evil's neighborhood?"
So said your shrewdness: true—so did not say
That other sort of theorists who held
Mere unintelligence prepared the way
For either seed's upsprouting: you repelled
Their notion that both kinds could sow themselves.
True! but admit 't is understanding delves
And drops each germ, what else but folly thwarts
The doer's settled purpose? Let the sage
Concede a use to evil, though there starts
Full many a burgeon thence, to disengage
With thumb and finger lest it spoil the yield
Too much of good's main tribute! But our main
Tough-tendoned mandrake-monster—purge the field
Of him for once and all? It follows plain
Who set him there to grow beholds repealed
His primal law: his ordinance proves vain:
And what beseems a king who cannot reign,
But to drop sceptre valid arm should wield?


VI

"Still there 's a parable"—retorts my friend—
"Shows agriculture with a difference!

What of the crop and weeds which solely blend
Because, once planted, none may pluck them thence?
The Gardener contrived thus? Vain pretence!
An enemy it was who unawares
Ruined the wheat by interspersing tares.
Where 's our desiderated forethought? Where 's
Knowledge, where power and will in evidence?
'T is Man's-play merely! Craft foils rectitude,
Malignity defeats beneficence.
And grant, at very last of all, the feud
'Twixt good and evil ends, strange thoughts intrude
Though good be garnered safely, and good's foe
Bundled for burning. Thoughts steal: 'Even so—
Why grant tares leave to thus o'ertop, o'ertower
Their field-mate, boast the stalk and flaunt the flower,
Triumph one sunny minute? Knowledge, power,
And will thus worked?' Man's fancy makes the fault!
Man, with the narrow mind, must cram inside
His finite God's infinitude,—earth's vault
He bids comprise the heavenly far and wide,
Since Man may claim a right to understand
What passes understanding. So, succinct
And trimly set in order, to be scanned
And scrutinized, lo—the divine lies linked
Fast to the human, free to move as moves
Its proper match: awhile they keep the grooves,
Discreetly side by side together pace,
Till sudden comes a stumble incident
Likely enough to Man's weak-footed race,
And he discovers—wings in rudiment,
Such as he boasts, which full-grown, free-distent
Would lift him skyward, fail of flight while pent
Within humanity's restricted space.
Abjure each fond attempt to represent
The formless, the illimitable! Trace
No outline, try no hint of human face
Or form or hand!"


VII


Friend, here 's a tracing meant
To help a guess at truth you never knew.
Bend but those eyes now, using mind's eye too,
And note—sufficient for all purposes—
The ground-plan—map you long have yearned for—yes,
Make out in markings—more what artist can?—
Goethe's Estate in Weimar,—just a plan!

A is the House, and B the Garden-gate,
And C the Grass-plot—you 've the whole estate
Letter by letter, down to Y the Pond,
And Z the Pigsty. Do you look beyond
The algebraic signs, and captions say
"Is A the House? But where 's the Roof to A,
Where 's Door, where 's Window? Needs must House have such!"
Ay, that were folly. Why so very much
More foolish than our mortal purblind way
Of seeking in the symbol no mere point
To guide our gaze through what were else inane,
But things—their solid selves? "Is, joint by joint,
Orion man-like,—as these dots explain
His constellation? Flesh composed of suns—
How can such be?" exclaim the simple ones.
Look through the sign to the thing signified—
Shown nowise, point by point at best descried,
Each an orb's topmost sparkle: all beside
Its shine is shadow: turn the orb one jot—
Up flies the new flash to reveal 't was not
The whole sphere late flamboyant in your ken!


VIII

"What need of symbolizing? Fitlier men
Would take on tongue mere facts—few, faint and far,
Still facts not fancies: quite enough they are,
That Power, that Knowledge, and that Will,—add then
Immensity, Eternity: these jar
Nowise with our permitted thought and speech.
Why human attributes?"

A myth may teach:
Only, who better would expound it thus
Must be Euripides, not Æschylus.


IX

Boundingly up through Night's wall dense and dark,
Embattled crags and clouds, outbroke the Sun
Above the conscious earth, and one by one
Her heights and depths absorbed to the last spark
His fluid glory, from the far fine ridge
Of mountain-granite which, transformed to gold,
Laughed first the thanks back, to the vale's dusk fold
On fold of vapor-swathing, like a bridge

Shattered beneath some giant's stamp. Night wist
Her work done and betook herself in mist
To marsh and hollow, there to bide her time
Blindly in acquiescence. Everywhere
Did earth acknowledge Sun's embrace sublime,
Thrilling her to the heart of things: since there
No ore ran liquid, no spar branched anew,
No arrowy crystal gleamed, but straightway grew
Glad through the inrush—glad nor more nor less
Than, 'neath his gaze, forest and wilderness,
Hill, dale, land, sea, the whole vast stretch and spread,
The universal world of creatures bred
By Sun's munificence, alike gave praise—
All creatures but one only: gaze for gaze,
Joyless and thankless, who—all scowling can—
Protests against the innumerous praises? Man,
Sullen and silent.

Stand thou forth then, state
Thy wrong, thou sole aggrieved—disconsolate—
While every beast, bird, reptile, insect, gay
And glad acknowledges the bounteous day!


X


Man speaks now: "What avails Sun's earth-felt thrill
To me? Sun penetrates the ore, the plant—
They feel and grow: perchance with subtler skill
He interfuses fly, worm, brute, until
Each favored object pays life's ministrant
By pressing, in obedience to his will,
Up to completion of the task prescribed,
So stands and stays a type. Myself imbibed
Such influence also, stood and stand complete—
The perfect Man,—head, body, hands and feet,
True to the pattern: but does that suffice?
How of my superadded mind which needs
—Not to be, simply, but to do, and pleads
For—more than knowledge that by some device
Sun quickens matter: mind is nobly fain
To realize the marvel, make—for sense
As mind—the unseen visible, condense
—Myself—Sun's all-pervading influence
So as to serve the needs of mind, explain
What now perplexes. Let the oak increase
His corrugated strength on strength, the palm
Lift joint by joint her fan-fruit, ball and balm,—

Let the coiled serpent bask in bloated peace,—
The eagle, like some skyey derelict,
Drift in the blue, suspended, glorying,—
The lion lord it by the desert-spring,—
What know or care they of the power which pricked
Nothingness to perfection? I, instead,
When all-developed still am found a thing
All-incomplete: for what though flesh had force
Transcending theirs—hands able to unring
The tightened snake's coil, eyes that could out-course
The eagle's soaring, voice whereat the king
Of carnage couched discrowned? Mind seeks to see,
Touch, understand, by mind inside of me,
The outside mind—whose quickening I attain
To recognize—I only. All in vain
Would mind address itself to render plain
The nature of the essence. Drag what lurks
Behind the operation—that which works
Latently everywhere by outward proof—
Drag that mind forth to face mine? No! aloof
I solely crave that one of all the beams
Which do Sun's work in darkness, at my will
Should operate—myself for once have skill
To realize the energy which streams
Flooding the universe. Above, around,
Beneath—why mocks that mind my own thus found
Simply of service, when the world grows dark,
To half-surmise—were Sun's use understood,
I might demonstrate him supplying food,
Warmth, life, no less the while? To grant one spark
Myself may deal with—make it thaw my blood
And prompt my steps, were truer to the mark
Of mind's requirement than a half-surmise
That somehow secretly is operant,
A power all matter feels, mind only tries
To comprehend! Once more—no idle vaunt
'Man comprehends the Sun's self!' Mysteries
At source why probe into? Enough: display,
Make demonstrable, how, by night as day,
Earth's centre and sky's outspan, all 's informed
Equally by Sun's efflux!—source from whence
If just one spark I drew, full evidence
Were mine of fire ineffably enthroned—
Sun's self made palpable to Man!"

Thus moaned
Man till Prometheus helped him,—as we learn,—
Offered an artifice whereby he drew
Sun's rays into a focus,—plain and true,
The very Sun in little: made fire burn
And henceforth do Man service—glass-conglobed
Though to a pin-point circle—all the same
Comprising the Sun's self, but Sun disrobed
Of that else-unconceived essential flame
Borne by no naked sight. Shall mind's eye strive
Achingly to companion as it may
The supersubtle effluence, and contrive
To follow beam and beam upon their way
Hand-breadth by hand-breadth, till sense faint—confessed
Frustrate, eluded by unknown unguessed
Infinitude of action? Idle quest!
Rather ask aid from optics. Sense, descry
The spectrum—mind, infer immensity!
Little?  In little, light, warmth, life are blessed—
Which, in the large, who sees to bless? Not I
More than yourself: so, good my friend, keep still
Trustful with—me? with thee, sage Mandeville!


WITH DANIEL BARTOLI

I


Don, the divinest women that have walked
Our world were scarce those saints of whom we talked.
My saint, for instance—worship if you will!
'T is pity poets need historians' skill:
What legendary 's worth a chronicle?


II


Come, now! A great lord once upon a time
Visited—oh a king, of kings the prime,
To sign a treaty such as never was:
For the king's minister had brought to pass
That this same duke—so style him—must engage
Two of his dukedoms as an heritage
After his death to this exorbitant
Craver of kingship. "Let who lacks go scant,
Who owns much, give the more to!" Why rebuke?
So bids the devil, so obeys the duke.

III

Now, as it happened, at his sister's house
—Duchess herself—indeed the very spouse
Of the king's uncle,—while the deed of gift
Whereby our duke should cut his rights adrift
Was drawing, getting ripe to sign and seal—
What does the frozen heart but uncongeal
And, shaming his transcendent kin and kith,
Whom do the duke's eyes make acquaintance with?
A girl. "What, sister, may this wonder be?"
"Nobody! Good as beautiful is she,
With gifts that match her goodness, no faint flaw
I' the white: she were the pearl you think you saw,
But that she is—what corresponds to white?
Some other stone, the true pearl's opposite,
As cheap as pearls are costly. She 's—now, guess
Her parentage! Once—twice—thrice? Foiled, confess!
Drugs, duke, her father deals in—faugh, the scents!—
Manna and senna—such medicaments
For payment he compounds you. Stay—stay—stay!
I 'll have no rude speech wrong her! Whither away,
The hot-head? Ah, the scapegrace! She deserves
Respect—compassion, rather! right it serves
My folly, trusting secrets to a fool!
Already at it, is he? She keeps cool—
Helped by her fan's spread. Well, our state atones
For thus much license, and words break no bones!"
(Hearts, though, sometimes.)


IV

Next morn 't was "Reason, rate,
Rave, sister, on till doomsday! Sure as fate,
I wed that woman—what a woman is
Now that I know, who never knew till this!"
So swore the duke. "I wed her: once again—
Rave, rate, and reason—spend your breath in vain!"


V

At once was made a contract firm and fast,
Published the banns were, only marriage, last,
Required completion when the Church's rite

Should bless and bid depart, make happy quite
The coupled man and wife forevermore:
Which rite was soon to follow. Just before—
All things at all but end—the folk o' the bride
Flocked to a summons. Pomp the duke defied:
"Of ceremony—so much as empowers,
Naught that exceeds, suits best a tie like ours"—
He smiled—"all else were mere futility.
We vow, God hears us: God and you and I—
Let the world keep at distance! This is why
We choose the simplest forms that serve to bind
Lover and lover of the human kind,
No care of what degree—of kings or clowns—
Come blood and breeding. Courtly smiles and frowns
Miss of their mark, would idly soothe or strike
My style and yours—in one style merged alike—
God's man and woman merely. Long ago
'T was rounded in my ears 'Duke, wherefore slow
To use a privilege? Needs must one who reigns
Pay reigning's due: since statecraft so ordains—
Wed for the commonweal's sake! law prescribes
One wife: but to submission license bribes
Unruly nature: mistresses accept
—Well, at discretion!' Prove I so inept
A scholar, thus instructed? Dearest, be
Wife and all mistresses in one to me,
Now, henceforth, and forever!" So smiled he.


VI

Good: but the minister, the crafty one,
Got ear of what was doing—all but done—
Not sooner, though, than the king's very self,
Warned by the sister on how sheer a shelf
Royalty's ship was like to split. "I bar
The abomination! Mix with muck my star?
Shall earth behold prodigiously enorbed
An upstart marsh-born meteor sun-absorbed?
Nuptial me no such nuptials!" "Past dispute,
Majesty speaks with wisdom absolute,"
Admired the minister: "yet, all the same,
I would we may not—while we play his game,
The ducal meteor's—also lose our own,
The solar monarch's: we relieve your throne
Of an ungracious presence, like enough:
Balked of his project he departs in huff,
And so cuts short—dare I remind the king?—

Our not so unsuccessful bargaining.
The contract for eventual heritage
Happens to pari passu reach the stage
Attained by just this other contract,—each
Unfixed by signature though fast in speech.
Off goes the duke in dudgeon—off withal
Go with him his two dukedoms past recall.
You save a fool from tasting folly's fruit,
Obtain small thanks thereby, and lose to boot
Sagacity's reward. The jest is grim:
The man will mulct you—for amercing him?
Nay, for ... permit a poor similitude!
A witless wight in some fantastic mood
Would drown himself: you plunge into the wave,
Pluck forth the undeserving: he, you save,
Pulls you clean under also for your pains.
Sire, little need that I should tax my brains
To help your inspiration!" "Let him sink!
Always contriving"—hints the royal wink—
"To keep ourselves dry while we claim his clothes."


VII

Next day, the appointed day for plighting troths
At eve,—so little time to lose, you see,
Before the Church should weld, indissolubly
Bond into bond, wed these who, side by side,
Sit each by other, bold groom, blushing bride,—
At the preliminary banquet, graced
By all the lady's kinsfolk come in haste
To share her triumph,—lo, a thunderclap!
"Who importunes now?" "Such is my mishap—
In the king's name! No need that any stir
Except this lady!" bids the minister:
"With her I claim a word apart, no more:
For who gainsays—a guard is at the door.
Hold, duke! Submit you, lady, as I bow
To him whose mouthpiece speaks his pleasure now!
It well may happen I no whit arrest
Your marriage: be it so,—we hope the best!
By your leave, gentles! Lady, pray you, hence!
Duke, with my soul and body's deference!"


VIII

Doors shut, mouth opens and persuasion flows

Copiously forth. "What flesh shall dare oppose
The king's command? The matter in debate
—How plain it is! Yourself shall arbitrate,
Determine. Since the duke affects to rate
His prize in you beyond all goods of earth,
Accounts as naught old gains of rank and birth,
Ancestral obligation, recent fame,
(We know his feats)—nay, ventures to disclaim
Our will and pleasure almost—by report—
Waives in your favor dukeliness, in short,—
We—('t is the king speaks)—who might forthwith stay
Such suicidal purpose, brush away
A bad example shame would else record,—
Lean to indulgence rather. At his word
We take the duke: allow him to complete
The cession of his dukedoms, leave our feet
Their footstool when his own head, safe in vault,
Sleeps sound. Nay, would the duke repair his fault
Handsomely, and our forfeited esteem
Recover,—what if wisely he redeem
The past,—in earnest of good faith, at once
Give us such jurisdiction for the nonce
As may suffice—prevent occasion slip—
And constitute our actual ownership?
Concede this—straightway be the marriage blessed
By warrant of this paper! Things at rest,
This paper duly signed, down drops the bar,
To-morrow you become—from what you are,
The druggist's daughter—not the duke's mere spouse,
But the king's own adopted: heart and house
Open to you—the idol of a court
'Which heaven might copy'—sing our poet-sort.
In this emergency, on you depends
The issue: plead what bliss the king intends!
Should the duke frown, should arguments and prayers,
Nay, tears if need be, prove in vain,—who cares?
We leave the duke to his obduracy,
Companionless,—you, madam, follow me
Without, where divers of the body-guard
Wait signal to enforce the king's award
Of strict seclusion: over you at least
Vibratingly the sceptre threats increased
Precipitation! How avert its crash?"


IX


"Re-enter, sir! A hand that 's calm, not rash,

Averts it!" quietly the lady said.
"Yourself shall witness."
                    At the table's head
Where, mid the hushed guests, still the duke sat glued
In blank bewilderment, his spouse pursued
Her speech to end—syllabled quietude.


X

"Duke, I, your duchess of a day, could take
The hand you proffered me for love's sole sake,
Conscious my love matched yours; as you, myself
Would waive, when need were, all but love—from pelf
To potency. What fortune brings about
Haply in some far future, finds me out,
Faces me on a sudden here and now.
The better! Read—if beating heart allow—
Read this, and bid me rend to rags the shame!
I and your conscience—hear and grant our claim!
Never dare alienate God's gift you hold
Simply in trust for him! Choose muck for gold?
Could you so stumble in your choice, cajoled
By what I count my least of worthiness
—The youth, the beauty,—you renounce them—yes,
With all that's most too: love as well you lose,
Slain by what slays in you the honor! Choose!
Dear—yet my husband—dare I love you yet?"


XI

How the duke's wrath o'erboiled,—words, words, and yet
More words,—I spare you such fool's fever-fret.
They were not of one sort at all, one size,
As souls go—he and she. 'T is said, the eyes
Of all the lookers-on let tears fall fast.
The minister was mollified at last:
"Take a day,—two days even, ere through pride
You perish,—two days' counsel—then decide!"


XII

"If I shall save his honor and my soul?
Husband,—this one last time,—you tear the scroll?
Farewell, duke! Sir, I follow in your train!"

So she went forth: they never met again,
The duke and she. The world paid compliment
(Is it worth noting?) when, next day, she sent
Certain gifts back—"jewelry fit to deck
Whom you call wife." I know not round what neck
They took, to sparkling, in good time—weeks thence.


XIV

Of all which was the pleasant consequence,
So much and no more—that a fervid youth,
Big-hearted boy,—but ten years old, in truth—
Laid this to heart and loved, as boyhood can,
The unduchessed lady: boy and lad grew man:
He loved as man perchance may: did meanwhile
Good soldier-service, managed to beguile
The years, no few, until he found a chance:
Then, as at trumpet-summons to advance,
Outbroke the love that stood at arms so long,
Brooked no withstanding longer. They were wed.
Whereon from camp and court alike he fled,
Renounced the sun-king, dropped off into night,
Evermore lost, a ruined satellite:
And, oh, the exquisite deliciousness
That lapped him in obscurity! You guess
Such joy is fugitive: she died full soon.
He did his best to die—as sun, so moon
Left him, turned dusk to darkness absolute.
Failing of death—why, saintship seemed to suit:
Yes, your sort, Don! He trembled on the verge
Of monkhood: trick of cowl and taste of scourge
He tried: then, kicked not at the pricks perverse,
But took again, for better or for worse,
The old way in the world, and, much the same
Man o' the outside, fairly played life's game.


XV

"Now, Saint Scholastica, what time she fared
In Paynimrie, behold, a lion glared
Right in her path! Her waist she promptly strips
Of girdle, binds his teeth within his lips,
And, leashed all lamblike, to the Soldan's court

Leads him." Ay, many a legend of the sort
Do you praiseworthily authenticate:
Spare me the rest. This much of no debate
Admits: my lady flourished in grand days
When to be duchess was to dance the hays
Up, down, across the heaven amid its host:
While to be hailed the sun's own self almost—
So close the kinship—was—was—

Saint, for this.
Be yours the feet I stoop to—kneel and kiss!
So human? Then the mouth too, if you will!
Thanks to no legend but a chronicle.


XVI


One leans to like the duke, too: up we 'll patch
Some sort of saintship for him—not to match
Hers—but man's best and woman's worst amount
So nearly to the same thing, that we count
In man a miracle of faithfulness
If, while unfaithful somewhat, he lay stress
On the main fact that love, when love indeed,
Is wholly solely love from first to last—
Truth—all the rest a lie. Too likely, fast
Enough that necklace went to grace the throat
—Let 's say, of such a dancer as makes doat
The senses when the soul is satisfied—
Trogalia, say the Greeks—a sweetmeat tried
Approvingly by sated tongue and teeth,
Once body's proper meal consigned beneath
Such unconsidered munching.


XVII


Fancy's flight
Makes me a listener when, some sleepless night,
The duke reviewed his memories, and aghast
Found that the Present intercepts the Past
With such effect as when a cloud enwraps
The moon and, moon-suf£used, plays moon perhaps
To who walks under, till comes, late or soon,
A stumble: up he looks, and lo, the moon
Calm, clear, convincingly herself once more!
How could he 'scape the cloud that thrust between
Him and effulgence? Speak, fool—duke, I mean!

"Who bade you come, brisk-marching bold she-shape,
A terror with those black-balled worlds of eyes,
That black hair bristling solid-built from nape
To crown its coils about? O dread surmise!
Take, tread on, trample under past escape
Your capture, spoil and trophy! Do—devise
Insults for one who, fallen once, ne'er shall rise!

"Mock on, triumphant o'er the prostrate shame!
Laugh 'Here lies he among the false to Love—
Love's loyal liegeman once: the very same
Who, scorning his weak fellows, towered above
Inconstancy: yet why his faith defame?
Our eagle's victor was at least no dove,
No dwarfish knight picked up our giant's glove—

"'When, putting prowess to the proof, faith urged
Her champion to the challenge: had it chanced
That merely virtue, wisdom, beauty—merged
All in one woman—merely these advanced
Their claim to conquest,—hardly had he purged
His mind of memories, dearnesses enhanced
Rather than harmed by death, nor, disentranced,

"'Promptly had he abjured the old pretence
To prove his kind's superior—first to last
Display erect on his heart's eminence
An altar to the never-dying Past.
For such feat faith might boast fit play of fence
And easily disarm the iconoclast
Called virtue, wisdom, beauty: impudence

"'Fought in their stead, and how could faith but fall?
There came a bold she-shape brisk-marching, bent
No inch of her imperious stature, tall
As some war-engine from whose top was sent
One shattering volley out of eye's black ball,
And prone lay faith's defender!' Mockery spent?
Malice discharged in full? In that event,

"My queenly impudence, I cover close,
I wrap me round with love of your black hair,
Black eyes, black every wicked inch of those
Limbs' war-tower tallness: so much truth lives there

'Neath the dead heap of lies. And yet—who knows?
What if such things are? No less, such things were,
Then was the man your match whom now you dare

"Treat as existent still. A second truth!
They held—this heap of lies you rightly scorn—
A man who had approved himself in youth
More than a match for—you? for sea-foam born
Venus herself: you conquer him forsooth?
'T is me his ghost: he died since left and lorn,
As needs must Samson when his hair is shorn.

"Some day, and soon, be sure himself will rise,
Called into life by her who long ago
Left his soul whiling time in flesh-disguise.
Ghosts tired of waiting can play tricks, you know!
Tread, trample me—such sport we ghosts devise,
Waiting the morn-star's reappearance—though
You think we vanish scared by the cock's crow."


WITH CHRISTOPHER SMART

I


It seems as if ... or did the actual chance
Startle me and perplex? Let truth be said!
How might this happen? Dreaming, blindfold led
By visionary hand, did soul's advance
Precede my body's, gain inheritance
Of fact by fancy—so that when I read
At length with waking eyes your Song, instead
Of mere bewilderment, with me first glance
Was but full recognition that in trance
Or merely thought's adventure some old day
Of dim and done-with boyishness, or—well,
Why might it not have been, the miracle
Broke on me as I took my sober way
Through veritable regions of our earth
And made discovery, many a wondrous one?


II


Anyhow, fact or fancy, such its birth:
I was exploring some huge house, had gone
Through room and room complacently, no dearth

Anywhere of the signs of decent taste,
Adequate culture: wealth had run to waste
Nowise, nor penury was proved by stint:
All showed the Golden Mean without a hint
Of brave extravagance that breaks the rule.
The master of the mansion was no fool
Assuredly, no genius just as sure!
Safe mediocrity had scorned the lure
Of now too much and now too little cost,
And satisfied me sight was never lost
Of moderate design's accomplishment
In calm completeness. On and on I went
With no more hope than fear of what came next,
Till lo, I push a door, sudden uplift
A hanging, enter, chance upon a shift
Indeed of scene! So—thus it is thou deck'st
High heaven, our low earth's brick-and-mortar work?


III

It was the Chapel. That a star, from murk
Which hid, should flashingly emerge at last,
Were small surprise: but from broad day I passed
Into a presence that turned shine to shade.
There fronted me the Rafael Mother-Maid,
Never to whom knelt votarist in shrine
By Nature's bounty helped, by Art's divine
More varied—beauty with magnificence—
Than this: from floor to roof one evidence
Of how far earth may rival heaven. No niche
Where glory was not prisoned to enrich
Man's gaze with gold and gems, no space but glowed
With color, gleamed with carving—hues which owed
Their outburst to a brush the painter fed
With rainbow-substance—rare shapes never wed
To actual flesh and blood, which, brain-born once,
Became the sculptor's dowry, Art's response
To earth's despair. And all seemed old yet new:
Youth,—in the marble's curve, the canvas' hue,
Apparent,—wanted not the crowning thrill
Of age the consecrator. Hands long still
Had worked here—could it be, what lent them skill
Retained a power to supervise, protect,
Enforce new lessons with the old, connect
Our life with theirs? No merely modern touch
Told me that here the artist, doing much,
Elsewhere did more, perchance does better, lives—

So needs must learn.

## IV

Well, these provocatives
Having fulfilled their office, forth I went
Big with anticipation—well-nigh fear—
Of what next room and next for startled eyes
Might have in store, surprise beyond surprise.
Next room and next and next—what followed here?
Why, nothing! not one object to arrest
My passage—everywhere too manifest
The previous decent null and void of best
And worst, mere ordinary right and fit,
Calm commonplace which neither missed, nor hit
Inch-high, inch-low, the placid mark proposed.

Armed with this instance, have I diagnosed
Your case, my Christopher? The man was sound
And sane at starting: all at once the ground
Gave way beneath his step, a certain smoke
Curled up and caught him, or perhaps down broke
A fireball wrapping flesh and spirit both
In conflagration. Then—as heaven were loth
To linger—let earth understand too well
How heaven at need can operate—off fell
The flame-robe, and the untransfigured man
Resumed sobriety,—as he began,
So did he end nor alter pace, not he!

Now, what I fain would know is—could it be
That he—whoe'er he was that furnished forth
The Chapel, making thus, from South to North,
Rafael touch Leighton, Michelagnolo
Join Watts, was found but once combining so
The elder and the younger, taking stand
On Art's supreme,—or that yourself who sang
A Song where flute-breath silvers trumpet-clang,
And stations you for once on either hand
With Milton and with Keats, empowered to claim
Affinity on just one point—(or blame

Or praise my judgment, thus it fronts you full)—
How came it you resume the void and null,
Subside to insignificance,—live, die
—Proved plainly two mere mortals who drew nigh
One moment—that, to Art's best hierarchy,
This, to the superhuman poet-pair?
What if, in one point only, then and there
The otherwise all-unapproachable
Allowed impingement? Does the sphere pretend
To span the cube's breadth, cover end to end
The plane with its embrace? No, surely! Still,
Contact is contact, sphere's touch no whit less
Than cube's superimposure. Such success
Befell Smart only out of throngs between
Milton and Keats that donned the singing-dress—
Smart, solely of such songmen, pierced the screen
'Twixt thing and word, lit language straight from soul,—
Left no fine film-flake on the naked coal
Live from the censer—shapely or uncouth,
Fire-suffused through and through, one blaze of truth
Undeadened by a lie,—(you have my mind)—
For, think! this blaze outleapt with black behind
And blank before, when Hayley and the rest ...
But let the dead successors worst and best
Bury their dead: with life be my concern—
Yours with the fire-flame: what I fain would learn
Is just—(suppose me haply ignorant
Down to the common knowledge, doctors vaunt)
Just this—why only once the fire-flame was:
No matter if the marvel came to pass
The way folk judged—if power too long suppressed
Broke loose and maddened, as the vulgar guessed
Or simply brain-disorder (doctors said),
A turmoil of the particles disturbed,
Brain's workaday performance in your head,
Spurred spirit to wild action health had curbed,
And so verse issued in a cataract
Whence prose, before and after, unperturbed
Was wont to wend its way. Concede the fact
That here a poet was who always could—
Never before did—never after would—
Achieve the feat: how were such fact explained?


VII


Was it that when, by rarest chance, there fell
Disguise from Nature, so that Truth remained

Naked, and whoso saw for once could tell
Us others of her majesty and might
In large, her lovelinesses infinite
In little,—straight you used the power wherewith
Sense, penetrating as through rind to pith
Each object, thoroughly revealed might view
And comprehend the old things thus made new,
So that while eye saw, soul to tongue could trust
Thing which struck word out, and once more adjust
Real vision to right language, till heaven's vault
Pompous with sunset, storm-stirred sea's assault
On the swilled rock-ridge, earth's embosomed brood
Of tree and flower and weed, with all the life
That flies or swims or crawls, in peace or strife,
Above, below,—each had its note and name
For Man to know by,—Man who, now—the same
As erst in Eden, needs that all he sees
Be named him ere he note by what degrees
Of strength and beauty to its end Design
Ever thus operates—(your thought and mine,
No matter for the many dissident)—
So did you sing your Song, so truth found vent
In words for once with you?

VIII

Then—back was furled
The robe thus thrown aside, and straight the world
Darkened into the old oft-catalogued
Repository of things that sky, wave, land,
Or show or hide, clear late, accretion-clogged
Now, just as long ago, by tellings and
Re-tellings to satiety, which strike
Muffled upon the ear's drum. Very like
None was so startled as yourself when friends
Came, hailed your fast-returning wits: "Health mends
Importantly, for—to be plain with you—
This scribble on the wall was done—in lieu
Of pen and paper—with—ha, ha!—your key
Denting it on the wainscot! Do you see
How wise our caution was? Thus much we stopped
Of babble that had else grown print: and lopped
From your trim bay-tree this unsightly bough—
Smart's who translated Horace!  Write us now" ...
Why, what Smart did write—never afterward
One line to show that he, who paced the sward,
Had reached the zenith from his madhouse cell.

Was it because you judged (I know full well
You never had the fancy)—judged—as some—
That who makes poetry must reproduce
Thus ever and thus only, as they come,
Each strength, each beauty, everywhere diffuse
Throughout creation, so that eye and ear,
Seeing and hearing, straight shall recognize,
At touch of just a trait, the strength appear,—
Suggested by a line's lapse see arise
All evident the beauty,—fresh surprise
Startling at fresh achievement? "So, indeed,
Wallows the whale's bulk in the waste of brine,
Nor otherwise its feather-tufts make fine
Wild Virgin's Bower when stars faint off to seed!"
(My prose—your poetry I dare not give,
Purpling too much my mere gray argument.)
—Was it because you judged—when fugitive
Was glory found, and wholly gone and spent
Such power of startling up deaf ear, blind eye,
At truth's appearance,—that you humbly bent
The head and, bidding vivid work good-by,
Doffed lyric dress and trod the world once more
A drab-clothed decent proseman as before?
Strengths, beauties, by one word's flash thus laid bare
—That was effectual service: made aware
Of strengths and beauties, Man but hears the text,
Awaits your teaching. Nature? What comes next?
Why all the strength and beauty?—to be shown
Thus in one word's flash, thenceforth let alone
By Man who needs must deal with aught that 's known
Never so lately and so little? Friend,
First give us knowledge, then appoint its use!
Strength, beauty are the means: ignore their end?
As well you stopped at proving how profuse
Stones, sticks, nay stubble lie to left and right
Ready to help the builder,—careless quite
If he should take, or leave the same to strew
Earth idly,—as by word's flash bring in view
Strength, beauty, then bid who beholds the same
Go on beholding. Why gains unemployed?
Nature was made to be by Man enjoyed
First; followed duly by enjoyment's fruit,
Instruction—haply leaving joy behind:
And you, the instructor, would you slack pursuit

Of the main prize, as poet help mankind
Just to enjoy, there leave them? Play the fool,
Abjuring a superior privilege?
Please simply when your function is to rule—
By thought incite to deed? From edge to edge
Of earth's round, strength and beauty everywhere
Pullulate—and must you particularize
All, each and every apparition? Spare
Yourself and us the trouble! Ears and eyes
Want so much strength and beauty, and no less
Nor more, to learn life's lesson by. Oh, yes—
The other method 's favored in our day!
The end ere the beginning: as you may
Master the heavens before you study earth,
Make you familiar with the meteor's birth
Ere you descend to scrutinize the rose!
I say, o'erstep no least one of the rows
That lead man from the bottom where he plants
Foot first of all, to life's last ladder-top:
Arrived there, vain enough will seem the vaunts
Of those who say—"We scale the skies, then drop
To earth—to find, how all things there are loth
To answer heavenly law: we understand
The meteor's course, and lo, the rose's growth—
How other than should be by law's command!"
Would not you tell such—"Friends, beware lest fume
Offuscate sense: learn earth first ere presume
To teach heaven legislation. Law must be
Active in earth or nowhere: earth you see,—
Or there or not at all, Will, Power and Love
Admit discovery,—as below, above
Seek next law's confirmation! But reverse
The order, where 's the wonder things grow worse
Than, by the law your fancy formulates,
They should be? Cease from anger at the fates
Which thwart themselves so madly. Live and learn,
Not first learn and then live, is our concern.


WITH GEORGE BUBB DODINGTON

I

Ah, George Bubb Dodington Lord Melcombe,—no,
Yours was the wrong way!—always understand,
Supposing that permissibly you planned
How statesmanship—your trade—in outward show

Might figure as inspired by simple zeal
For serving country, king and commonweal,
(Though service tire to death the body, tease
The soul from out an o'ertasked patriot-drudge)
And yet should prove zeal's outward show agrees
In all respects—right reason being judge—
With inward care that, while the statesman spends
Body and soul thus freely for the sake
Of public good, his private welfare take
No harm by such devotedness. Intends
Scripture aught else—let captious folk inquire—
Which teaches "Laborers deserve their hire,
And who neglects his household bears the bell
Away of sinning from an infidel"?
Wiselier would fools that carp bestow a thought
How birds build nests; at outside, roughly wrought,
Twig knots with twig, loam plasters up each chink,
Leaving the inmate rudely lodged—you think?
Peep but inside!  That specious rude-and-rough
Covers a domicile where downy fluff
Embeds the ease-deserving architect,
Who toiled and moiled not merely to effect
'Twixt sprig and spray a stop-gap in the teeth
Of wind and weather, guard what swung beneath
From upset only, but contrived himself
A snug interior, warm and soft and sleek.
Of what material? Oh, for that, you seek
How nature prompts each volatile! Thus—pelf
Smoothens the human mudlark's lodging, power
Demands some hardier wrappage to embrace
Robuster heart-beats: rock, not tree nor tower,
Contents the building eagle: rook shoves close
To brother rook on branch, while crow morose
Apart keeps balance perched on topmost bough.
No sort of bird but suits his taste somehow:
Nay, Darwin tells of such as love the bower—
His bower-birds opportunely yield us yet
The lacking instance when at loss to get
A feathered parallel to what we find
The secret motor of some mighty mind
That worked such wonders—all for vanity!
Worked them to haply figure in the eye
Of intimates as first of—doers' kind?
Actors', that work in earnest sportively,
Paid by a sourish smile. How says the Sage?
Birds born to strut prepare a platform-stage
With sparkling stones and speckled shells, all sorts
Of slimy rubbish, odds and ends and orts,

Whereon to pose and posture and engage
The priceless female simper.


II

I have gone
Thus into detail, George Bubb Dodington,
Lest, when I take you presently to task
For the wrong way of working, you should ask
"What fool conjectures that profession means
Performance? that who goes behind the scenes
Finds,—acting over,—still the soot-stuff screens
Othello's visage, still the self-same cloak's
Bugle-bright-blackness half reveals half chokes
Hamlet's emotion, as ten minutes since?"
No, each resumes his garb, stands—Moor or prince—
Decently draped: just so with statesmanship!
All outside show, in short, is sham—why wince?
Concede me—while our parley lasts! You trip
Afterwards—lay but this to heart! (there lurks
Somewhere in all of us a lump which irks
Somewhat the spriteliest-scheming brain that 's bent
On brave adventure, would but heart consent!)
—Here trip you, that—your aim allowed as right—
Your means thereto were wrong. Come, we, this night,
Profess one purpose, hold one principle,
Are at odds only as to—not the will
But way of winning solace for ourselves
—No matter if the ore for which zeal delves
Be gold or coprolite, while zeal's pretence
Is—we do good to men at—whose expense
But ours? who tire the body, tease the soul,
Simply that, running, we may reach fame's goal
And wreathe at last our brows with bay—the State's
Disinterested slaves, nay—please the Fates—
Saviors and nothing less: such lot has been!
Statesmanship triumphs pedestalled, serene,—
O happy consummation!—brought about
By managing with skill the rabble-rout
For which we labor (never mind the name—
People or populace, for praise or blame)
Making them understand—their heaven, their hell,
Their every hope and fear is ours as well.
Man's cause—what other can we have at heart?
Whence follows that the necessary part
High o'er Man's head we play,—and freelier breathe
Just that the multitude which gasps beneath

May reach the level where unstifled stand
Ourselves at vantage to put forth a hand,
Assist the prostrate public. 'T is by right
Merely of such pretence, we reach the height
Where storms abound, to brave—nay, court their stress,
Though all too well aware—of pomp the less,
Of peace the more! But who are we, to spurn
For peace' sake, duty's pointing? Up, then—earn
Albeit no prize we may but martyrdom!
Now, such fit height to launch salvation from,
How get and gain? Since help must needs be craved
By would-be saviours of the else-unsaved,
How coax them to co-operate, lend a lift,
Kneel down and let us mount?


III

You say, "Make shift
By sham—the harsh word: preach and teach, persuade
Somehow the Public—not despising aid
Of salutary artifice—we seek
Solely their good: our strength would raise the weak,
Our cultivated knowledge supplement
Their rudeness, rawness: why to us were lent
Ability except to come in use?
Who loves his kind must by all means induce
That kind to let his love play freely, press
In Man's behalf to full performance!"


IV

Yes—
Yes, George, we know!—whereat they hear, believe,
And bend the knee, and on the neck receive
Who fawned and cringed to purpose? Not so, George!
Try simple falsehood on shrewd folk who forge
Lies of superior fashion day by day
And hour by hour? With craftsmen versed as they
What chance of competition when the tools
Only a novice wields? Are knaves such fools?
Disinterested patriots, spare your tongue
The tones thrice-silvery, cheek save smiles it flung
Pearl-like profuse to swine—a herd, whereof
No unit needs be taught, his neighbor's trough
Scarce holds for who but grunts and whines the husks
Due to a wrinkled snout that shows sharp tusks.

No animal—much less our lordly Man—
Obeys its like: with strength all rule began,
The stoutest awes the pasture. Soon succeeds
Discrimination,—nicer power Man needs
To rule him than is bred of bone and thew:
Intelligence must move strength's self. This too
Lasts but its time: the multitude at length
Looks inside for intelligence and strength
And finds them here and there to pick and choose:
"All at your service, mine, see!" Ay, but who 's
My George, at this late day, to make his boast
"In strength, intelligence, I rule the roast,
Beat, all and some, the ungraced who crowd your ranks?"
"Oh, but I love, would lead you, gain your thanks
By unexampled yearning for Man's sake—
Passion that solely waits your help to take
Effect in action!" George, which one of us
But holds with his own heart communion thus:
"I am, if not of men the first and best,
Still—to receive enjoyment—properest:
Which since by force I cannot, nor by wit
Most likely—craft must serve in place of it.
Flatter, cajole! If so I bring within
My net the gains which wit and force should win,
What hinders?" 'T is a trick we know of old:
Try, George, some other of tricks manifold!
The multitude means mass and mixture—right!
Are mixtures simple, pray, or composite?
Dive into Man, your medley: see the waste!
Sloth-stifled genius, energy disgraced
By ignorance, high aims with sorry skill,
Will without means and means in want of will
—Sure we might fish, from out the mothers' sons
That welter thus, a dozen Dodingtons!
Why call up Dodington, and none beside,
To take his seat upon our backs and ride
As statesman conquering and to conquer? Well,
The last expedient, which must needs excel
Those old ones—this it is,—at any rate
To-day's conception thus I formulate:
As simple force has been replaced, just so
Must simple wit be: men have got to know
Such wit as what you boast is nowise held
The wonder once it was, but, paralleled
Too plentifully, counts not,—puts to shame
Modest possessors like yourself who claim,
By virtue of it merely, power and place
—Which means the sweets of office. Since our race

Teems with the like of you, some special gift,
Your very own, must coax our hands to lift,
And backs to bear you: is it just and right
To privilege your nature?


V


"State things quite
Other than so"—make answer! "I pretend
No such community with men. Perpend
My key to domination! Who would use
Man for his pleasure needs must introduce
The element that awes Man. Once for all,
His nature owns a Supernatural
In fact as well as phrase—which found must he
—Where, in this doubting age? Old mystery
Has served its turn—seen through and sent adrift
To nothingness: new wizard-craft makes shift
Nowadays shorn of help by robe and book,—
Otherwise, elsewhere, for success must look
Than chalked-ring, incantation-gibberish.
Somebody comes to conjure: that 's he? Pish!
He 's like the roomful of rapt gazers,—there 's
No sort of difference in the garb he wears
From ordinary dressing,—gesture, speech,
Deportment, just like those of all and each
That eye their master of the minute. Stay!
What of the something—call it how you may—
Uncanny in the—quack? That 's easy said!
Notice how the Professor turns no head
And yet takes cognizance of who accepts,
Denies, is puzzled as to the adept's
Supremacy, yields up or lies in wait
To trap the trickster! Doubtless, out of date
Are dealings with the devil: yet, the stir
Of mouth, its smile half smug half sinister,
Mock-modest boldness masked in diffidence,—
What if the man have—who knows how or whence?—
Confederate potency unguessed by us—
Prove no such cheat as he pretends?"


VI


Ay, thus
Had but my George played statesmanship's new card
That carries all! "Since we"—avers the Bard—

"All of us have one human heart"—as good
As say—by all of us is understood
Right and wrong, true and false—in rough, at least,
We own a common conscience. God, man, beast—
How should we qualify the statesman-shape
I fancy standing with our world agape?
Disguise, flee, fight against with tooth and nail
The outrageous designation! "Quack" men quail
Before? You see, a little year ago
They heard him thunder at the thing which, lo,
To-day he vaunts for unscathed, while what erst
Heaven-high he lauded, lies hell-low, accursed!
And yet where 's change? Who, awe-struck, cares to point
Critical finger at a dubious joint
In armor, true as triplex, breast and back
Binding about, defiant of attack,
An imperturbability that 's—well,
Or innocence or impudence—how tell
One from the other? Could ourselves broach lies,
Yet brave mankind with those unaltered eyes,
Those lips that keep the quietude of truth?
Dare we attempt the like? What quick uncouth
Disturbance of thy smug economy,
O coward visage! Straight would all descry
Back on the man's brow the boy's blush once more!
No: he goes deeper—could our sense explore—
Finds conscience beneath conscience such as ours.
Genius is not so rare,—prodigious powers—
Well, others boast such,—but a power like this
Mendacious intrepidity—quid vis?
Besides, imposture plays another game,
Admits of no diversion from its aim
Of captivating hearts, sets zeal aflare
In every shape at every turn,—nowhere
Allows subsidence into ash. By stress
Of what does guile succeed but earnestness,
Earnest word, look and gesture? Touched with aught
But earnestness, the levity were fraught
With ruin to guile's film-work. Grave is guile;
Here no act wants its qualifying smile,
Its covert pleasantry to neutralize
The outward ardor. Can our chief despise
Even while most he seems to adulate?
As who should say "What though it be my fate
To deal with fools? Among the crowd must lurk
Some few with faculty to judge my work
Spite of its way which suits, they understand,
The crass majority:—the Sacred Band,

No duping them forsooth!" So tells a touch
Of subintelligential nod and wink—
Turning foes friends. Coarse flattery moves the gorge:
Mine were the mode to awe the many, George!
They guess you half despise them while most bent
On demonstrating that your sole intent
Strives for their service. Sneer at them? Yourself
'T is you disparage,—tricksy as an elf,
Scorning what most you strain to bring to pass,
Laughingly careless,—triply cased in brass,—
While pushing strenuous to the end in view.
What follows? Why, you formulate within
The vulgar headpiece this conception: "Win
A master-mind to serve us needs we must,
One who, from motives we but take on trust,
Acts strangelier—haply wiselier than we know
Stronglier, for certain. Did he say 'I throw
Aside my good for yours, in all I do
Care nothing for myself and all for you'—
We should both understand and disbelieve:
Said he, 'Your good I laugh at in my sleeve,
My own it is I solely labor at,
Pretending yours the while'—that, even that,
We, understanding well, give credence to,
And so will none of it. But here 't is through
Our recognition of his service, wage
Well earned by work, he mounts to such a stage
Above competitors as all save Bubb
Would agonize to keep. Yet—here 's the rub—
So slightly does he hold by our esteem
Which solely fixed him fast there, that we seem
Mocked every minute to our face, by gibe
And jest—scorn insuppressive: what ascribe
The rashness to? Our pay and praise to boot—
Do these avail him to tread under foot
Something inside us all and each, that stands
Somehow instead of somewhat which commands
'Lie not'? Folk fear to jeopardize their soul,
Stumble at times, walk straight upon the whole,—
That 's nature's simple instinct: what may be
The portent here, the influence such as we
Are strangers to?"—


VII

Exact the thing I call
Man's despot, just the Supernatural

Which, George, was wholly out of—far beyond
Your theory and practice. You had conned
But to reject the precept "To succeed
In gratifying selfishness and greed,
Asseverate such qualities exist
Nowise within yourself! then make acquist
By all means, with no sort of fear!" Alack,
That well-worn lie is obsolete! Fall back
On still a working pretext—"Hearth and Home,
The Altar, love of England, hate of Rome"—
That 's serviceable lying—that perchance
Had screened you decently: but 'ware advance
By one step more in perspicacity
Of these our dupes! At length they get to see
As through the earlier, this the latter plea—
And find the greed and selfishness at source!
Ventum est ad triarios: last resource
Should be to what but—exquisite disguise
Disguise-abjuring, truth that looks like lies,
Frankness so sure to meet with unbelief?
Say—you hold in contempt—not them in chief—
But first and foremost your own self! No use
In men but to make sport for you, induce
The puppets now to dance, now stand stock-still,
Now knock their heads together, at your will
For will's sake only—while each plays his part
Submissive: why? through terror at the heart:
"Can it be—this bold man, whose hand we saw
Openly pull the wires, obeys some law
Quite above Man's—nay, God's?" On face fall they.
This was the secret missed, again I say,
Out of your power to grasp conception of,
Much less employ to purpose. Hence the scoff
That greets your very name: folk see but one
Fool more, as well as knave, in Dodington.


WITH FRANCIS FURINI

I


Nay, that, Furini, never I at least
Mean to believe! What man you were I know,
While you walked Tuscan earth, a painter-priest,
Something about two hundred years ago.
Priest—you did duty punctual as the sun
That rose and set above Saint Sano's church,

Blessing Mugello: of your flock not one
But showed a whiter fleece because of smirch,
Your kind hands wiped it clear from: were they poor?
Bounty broke bread apace,—did marriage lag
For just the want of moneys that ensure
Fit hearth-and-home provision?—straight your bag
Unplumped itself,—reached hearts by way of palms
Goodwill's shake had but tickled. All about
Mugello valley, felt some parish qualms
At worship offered in bare walls without
The comfort of a picture?—prompt such need
Our painter would supply, and throngs to see
Witnessed that goodness—no unholy greed
Of gain—had coaxed from Don Furini—he
Whom princes might in vain implore to toil
For worldly profit—such a masterpiece.
Brief—priest, you poured profuse God's wine and oil
Praiseworthily, I know: shall praising cease
When, priestly vesture put aside, mere man,
You stand for judgment? Rather—what acclaim
—"Good son, good brother, friend in whom we scan
No fault nor flaw"—salutes Furini's name,
The loving as the liberal! Enough:
Only to ope a lily, though for sake
Of setting free its scent, disturbs the rough
Loose gold about its anther. I shall take
No blame in one more blazon, last of all—
Good painter were you: if in very deed
I styled you great—what modern art dares call
My word in question? Let who will take heed
Of what he seeks and misses in your brain
To balance that precision of the brush
Your hand could ply so deftly: all in vain
Strives poet's power for outlet when the push
Is lost upon a barred and bolted gate
Of painter's impotency. Agnolo—
Thine were alike the head and hand, by fate
Doubly endowed! Who boasts head only—woe
To hand's presumption should brush emulate
Fancy's free passage by the pen, and show
Thought wrecked and ruined where the inexpert
Foolhardy fingers half grasped, half let go
Film-wings the poet's pen arrests unhurt!
No—painter such as that miraculous
Michael, who deems you? But the ample gift
Of gracing walls else blank of this our house
Of life with imagery, one bright drift
Poured forth by pencil,—man and woman mere,

Glorified till half owned for gods,—the dear
Fleshly perfection of the human shape,—
This was apportioned you whereby to praise
Heaven and bless earth. Who clumsily essays,
By slighting painter's craft, to prove the ape
Of poet's pen-creation, just betrays
Twofold ineptitude.


II

By such sure ways
Do I return, Furini, to my first
And central confidence—that he I proved
Good priest, good man, good painter, and rehearsed
Praise upon praise to show—not simply loved
For virtue, but for wisdom honored too
Needs must Furini be,—it follows—who
Shall undertake to breed in me belief
That, on his death-bed, weakness played the thief
With wisdom, folly ousted reason quite?
List to the chronicler! With main and might—
So fame runs—did the poor soul beg his friends
To buy and burn his hand-work, make amends
For having reproduced therein—(Ah me!
Sighs fame—that's friend Filippo)—nudity!
Yes, I assure you; he would paint—not men
Merely—a pardonable fault—but when
He had to deal with—oh, not mother Eve
Alone, permissibly in Paradise
Naked and unashamed,—but dared achieve
Dreadful distinction, at soul-safety's price,
By also painting women—(why the need?)
Just as God made them: there, you have the truth!
Yes, rosed from top to toe in flush of youth,
One foot upon the moss-fringe, would some Nymph
Try, with its venturous fellow, if the lymph
Were chillier than the slab-stepped fountain-edge;
The while a-heap her garments on its ledge
Of boulder lay within hand's easy reach,
—No one least kid-skin cast around her! Speech
Shrinks from enumerating case and case
Of—were it but Diana at the chase,
With tunic tucked discreetly hunting-high!
No, some Queen Venus set our necks awry,
Turned faces from the painter's all-too-frank
Triumph of flesh! For—whom had he to thank
—This self-appointed nature-student? Whence

Picked he up practice? By what evidence
Did he unhandsomely become adept
In simulating bodies? How except
By actual sight of such? Himself confessed
The enormity: quoth Philip, "When I pressed
The painter to acknowledge his abuse
Of artistry else potent—what excuse
Made the infatuated man? I give
His very words: 'Did you but know, as I,
—O scruple-splitting sickly-sensitive
Mild-moral-monger, what the agony
Of Art is ere Art satisfy herself
In imitating Nature—(Man, poor elf,
Striving to match the finger-mark of Him
The immeasurably matchless)—gay or grim,
Pray, would your smile be? Leave mere fools to tax
Art's high-strung brain's intentness as so lax
That, in its mid-throe, idle fancy sees
The moment for admittance!' Pleadings these—
Specious, I grant." So adds, and seems to wince
Somewhat, our censor—but shall truth convince
Blockheads like Baldinucci?


III

I resume
My incredulity: your other kind
Of soul, Furini, never was so blind,
Even through death-mist, as to grope in gloom
For cheer beside a bonfire piled to turn
Ashes and dust all that your noble life
Did homage to life's Lord by,—bid them burn
—These Baldinucci blockheads—pictures rife
With record, in each rendered loveliness,
That one appreciative creature's debt
Of thanks to the Creator, more or less,
Was paid according as heart's-will had met
Hand's-power in Art's endeavor to express
Heaven's most consummate of achievements, bless
Earth by a semblance of the seal God set
On woman his supremest work. I trust
Rather, Furini, dying breath had vent
In some fine fervor of thanksgiving just
For this—that soul and body's power you spent—
Agonized to adumbrate, trace in dust
That marvel which we dream the firmament
Copies in star-device when fancies stray

Outlining, orb by orb, Andromeda—
God's best of beauteous and magnificent
Revealed to earth—the naked female form.
Nay, I mistake not: wrath that's but lukewarm
Would boil indeed were such a critic styled
Himself an artist: artist! Ossa piled
Topping Olympus—the absurd which crowns
The extravagant—whereat one laughs, not frowns.
Paints he? One bids the poor pretender take
His sorry self, a trouble and disgrace,
From out the sacred presence, void the place
Artists claim only. What—not merely wake
Our pity that suppressed concupiscence—
A satyr masked as matron—makes pretence
To the coarse blue-fly's instinct—can perceive
No better reason why she should exist—
—God's lily-limbed and blushrose-bosomed Eve—
Than as a hot-bed for the sensualist
To fly-blow with his fancies, make pure stuff
Breed him back filth—this were not crime enough?
But further—fly to style itself—nay, more—
To steal among the sacred ones, crouch down
Though but to where their garments sweep the floor—
—Still catching some faint sparkle from the crown
Crowning transcendent Michael, Leonard,
Rafael,—to sit beside the feet of such,
Unspurned because unnoticed, then reward
Their toleration—mercy overmuch—
By stealing from the throne-step to the fools
Curious outside the gateway, all-agape
To learn by what procedure, in the schools
Of Art, a merest man in outward shape
May learn to be Correggio! Old and young,
These learners got their lesson: Art was just
A safety-screen—(Art, which Correggio's tongue
Calls "Virtue")—for a skulking vice: mere lust
Inspired the artist when his Night and Morn
Slept and awoke in marble on that edge
Of heaven above our awe-struck earth: lust-born
His Eve low bending took the privilege
Of life from what our eyes saw—God's own palm
That put the flame forth—to the love and thanks
Of all creation save this recreant!


IV

Calm

Our phrase, Furini! Not the artist-ranks
Claim riddance of an interloper: no—
This Baldinucci did but grunt and sniff
Outside Art's pale—ay, grubbed, where pine-trees grow,
For pignuts only.


V

You the Sacred! If
Indeed on you has been bestowed the dower
Of Art in fulness, graced with head and hand,
Head—to lookup not downwards, hand—of power
To make head's gain the portion of a world
Where else the uninstructed ones too sure
Would take all outside beauty—film that's furled
About a star—for the star's self, endure
No guidance to the central glory,—nay,
(Sadder) might apprehend the film was fog,
Or (worst) wish all but vapor well away,
And sky's pure product thickened from earth's bog—
Since so, nor seldom, have your worthiest failed
To trust their own soul's insight—why? except
For warning that the head of the adept
May too much prize the hand, work unassailed
By scruple of the better sense that finds
An orb within each halo, bids gross flesh
Free the fine spirit-pattern, nor enmesh
More than is meet a marvel, custom blinds
Only the vulgar eye to. Now, less fear
That you, the foremost of Art's fellowship,
Will oft—will ever so offend! But—hip
And thigh—smite the Philistine! You—slunk here—
Connived at, by too easy tolerance,
Not to scrape palette simply or squeeze brush,
But dub your very self an Artist? Tush—
You, of the daubings, is it, dare advance
This doctrine that the Artist-mind must needs
Own to affinity with yours—confess
Provocative acquaintance, more or less,
With each impurely-peevish worm that breeds
Inside your brain's receptacle?


VI

Enough.
Who owns "I dare not look on diadems

Without an itch to pick out, purloin gems
Others contentedly leave sparkling"—gruff
Answers the guard of the regalia: "Why—
Consciously kleptomaniac—thrust yourself
Where your illicit craving after pelf
Is tempted most—in the King's treasury?
Go elsewhere! Sort with thieves, if thus you feel—
When folk clean-handed simply recognize
Treasure whereof the mere sight satisfies—
But straight your fingers are on itch to steal!
Hence with you!"
Pray, Furini!

VII

"Bounteous God,
Deviser and dispenser of all gifts
To soul through sense,—in Art the soul uplifts
Man's best of thanks! What but thy measuring-rod
Meted forth heaven and earth? more intimate,
Thy very hands were busied with the task
Of making, in this human shape, a mask—
A match for that divine. Shall love abate
Man's wonder? Nowise! True—true—all too true—
No gift but, in the very plenitude
Of its perfection, goes maimed, misconstrued
By wickedness or weakness: still, some few
Have grace to see thy purpose, strength to mar
Thy work by no admixture of their own,
—Limn truth not falsehood, bid us love alone
The type untampered with, the naked star!"

VIII

And, prayer done, painter—what if you should preach?
Not as of old when playing pulpiteer
To simple-witted country folk, but here
In actual London try your powers of speech
On us the cultured, therefore skeptical—
What would you? For, suppose he has his word
In faith's behalf, no matter how absurd,
This painter-theologian? One and all
We lend an ear—nay, Science takes thereto—
Encourages the meanest who has racked
Nature until he gains from her some fact,
To state what truth is from his point of view,

Mere pin-point though it be: since many such
Conduce to make a whole, she bids our friend
Come forward unabashed and haply lend
His little life-experience to our much
Of modern knowledge. Since she so insists,
Up stands Furini.


IX

"Evolutionists!
At truth I glimpse from depths, you glance from heights,
Our stations for discovery opposites,—
How should ensue agreement? I explain:
'T is the tip-top of things to which you strain
Your vision, until atoms, protoplasm,
And what and whence and how may be the spasm
Which sets all going, stop you: down perforce
Needs must your observation take its course,
Since there 's no moving upwards: link by link
You drop to where the atoms somehow think.
Feel, know themselves to be: the world 's begun,
Such as we recognize it. Have you done
Descending? Here's ourself,—Man, known to-day,
Duly evolved at last,—so far, you say,
The sum and seal of being's progress. Good!
Thus much at least is clearly understood—
Of power does Man possess no particle:
Of knowledge—just so much as shows that still
It ends in ignorance on every side:
But righteousness—ah, Man is deified
Thereby, for compensation! Make survey
Of Man's surroundings, try creation—nay,
Try emulation of the minimized
Minuteness fancy may conceive! Surprised
Reason becomes by two defeats for one—
Not only power at each phenomenon
Baffled, but knowledge also in default—
Asking what is minuteness—yonder vault
Speckled with suns, or this the millionth—thing,
How shall I call?—that on some insect's wing
Helps to make out in dyes the mimic star?
Weak, ignorant, accordingly we are:
What then? The worse for Nature! Where began
Righteousness, moral sense except in Man?
True, he makes nothing, understands no whit:
Had the initiator-spasm seen fit
Thus doubly to endow him, none the worse

And much the better were the universe.
What does Man see or feel or apprehend
Here, there, and everywhere, but faults to mend,
Omissions to supply,—one wide disease
Of things that are, which Man at once would ease
Had will but power and knowledge? failing both—
Things must take will for deed—Man, nowise loth,
Accepts pre-eminency: mere blind force—
Mere knowledge undirected in its course
By any care for what is made or marred
In either's operation—these award
The crown to? Rather let it deck thy brows,
Man, whom alone a righteousness endows
Would cure the wide world's ailing!  Who disputes
Thy claim thereto? Had Spasm more attributes
Than power and knowledge in its gift, before
Man came to pass? The higher that we soar,
The less of moral sense like Man's we find:
No sign of such before,—what comes behind,
Who guesses! But until there crown our sight
The quite new—not the old mere infinite
Of changings,—some fresh kind of sun and moon,—
Then, not before, shall I expect a boon
Of intuition just as strange, which turns
Evil to good, and wrong to right, unlearns
All Man's experience learned since Man was he.
Accept in Man, advanced to this degree,
The Prime Mind, therefore! neither wise nor strong—
Whose fault? but were he both, then right, not wrong
As now, throughout the world were paramount
According to his will,—which I account
The qualifying faculty. He stands
Confessed supreme—the monarch whose commands
Could he enforce, how bettered were the world!
He's at the height this moment—to be hurled
Next moment to the bottom by rebound
Of his own peal of laughter. All around
Ignorance wraps him,—whence and how and why
Things are,—yet cloud breaks and lets blink the sky
Just overhead, not elsewhere! What assures
His optics that the very blue which lures
Comes not of black outside it, doubly dense?
Ignorance overwraps his moral sense,
Winds him about, relaxing, as it wraps,
So much and no more than lets through perhaps
The murmured knowledge—'Ignorance exists.'

X

"I at the bottom, Evolutionists,
Advise beginning, rather. I profess
To know just one fact—my self-consciousness,—
'Twixt ignorance and ignorance enisled,—
Knowledge: before me was my Cause—that 's styled
God: after, in due course succeeds the rest,—
All that my knowledge comprehends—at best—
At worst, conceives about in mild despair.
Light needs must touch on either darkness: where?
Knowledge so far impinges on the Cause
Before me, that I know—by certain laws
Wholly unknown, whate'er I apprehend
Within, without me, had its rise: thus blend
I, and all things perceived, in one Effect.
How far can knowledge any ray project
On what comes after me—the universe?
Well, my attempt to make the cloud disperse
Begins—not from above but underneath:
I climb, you soar,—who soars soon loses breath
And sinks, who climbs keeps one foot firm on fact
Ere hazarding the next step: soul's first act
(Call consciousness the soul—some name we need)
Getting itself aware, through stuff decreed
Thereto (so call the body)—who has stept
So far, there let him stand, become adept
In body ere he shift his station thence
One single hair's breadth. Do I make pretence
To teach, myself unskilled in learning? Lo,
My life's work! Let my pictures prove I know
Somewhat of what this fleshly frame of ours
Or is or should be, how the soul empowers
The body to reveal its every mood
Of love and hate, pour forth its plenitude
Of passion. If my hand attained to give
Thus permanence to truth else fugitive,
Did not I also fix each fleeting grace
Of form and feature—save the beauteous face—
Arrest decay in transitory might
Of bone and muscle—cause the world to bless
Forever each transcendent nakedness
Of man and woman? Were such feats achieved
By sloth, or strenuous labor unrelieved,
—Yet lavished vainly? Ask that underground
(So may I speak) of all on surface found
Of flesh-perfection! Depths on depths to probe
Of all-inventive artifice, disrobe

Marvel at hiding under marvel, pluck
Veil after veil from Nature—were the luck
Ours to surprise the secret men so name,
That still eludes the searcher—all the same,
Repays his search with still fresh proof—'Externe,
Not inmost, is the Cause, fool! Look and learn!'
Thus teach my hundred pictures: firm and fast
There did I plant my first foot. And the next?
Nowhere! 'T was put forth and withdrawn, perplexed
At touch of what seemed stable and proved stuff
Such as the colored clouds are: plain enough
There lay the outside universe: try Man—
My most immediate! and the dip began
From safe and solid into that profound
Of ignorance I tell you surges round
My rock-spit of self-knowledge. Well and ill,
Evil and good irreconcilable
Above, beneath, about my every side,—
How did this wild confusion far and wide
Tally with my experience when my stamp—
So far from stirring—struck out, each a lamp,
Spark after spark of truth from where I stood—
Pedestalled triumph? Evil there was good,
Want was the promise of supply, defect
Ensured completion,—where and when and how?
Leave that to the First Cause! Enough that now,
Here where I stand, this moment's me and mine,
Shows me what is, permits me to divine
What shall be. Wherefore? Nay, how otherwise?
Look at my pictures! What so glorifies
The body that the permeating soul
Finds there no particle elude control
Direct, or fail of duty,—most obscure
When most subservient? Did that Cause ensure
The soul such raptures as its fancy stings
Body to furnish when, uplift by wings
Of passion, here and now, it leaves the earth,
Loses itself above, where bliss has birth—
(Heaven, be the phrase)—did that same Cause contrive
Such solace for the body, soul must dive
At drop of fancy's pinion, condescend
To bury both alike on earth, our friend
And fellow, where minutely exquisite
Low lie the pleasures, now and here—no herb
But hides its marvel, peace no doubts perturb
In each small mystery of insect life—
—Shall the soul's Cause thus gift the soul, yet strife
Continue still of fears with hopes,—for why?

What if the Cause, whereof we now descry
So far the wonder-working, lack at last
Will, power, benevolence—a protoplast,
No consummator, sealing up the sum
Of all things,—past and present and to come—
Perfection? No, I have no doubt at all!
There's my amount of knowledge—great or small,
Sufficient for my needs: for see! advance
Its light now on that depth of ignorance
I shrank before from—yonder where the world
Lies wreck-strewn,—evil towering, prone good—hurled
From pride of place, on every side. For me
(Patience, beseech you!) knowledge can but be
Of good by knowledge of good's opposite—
Evil,—since, to distinguish wrong from right,
Both must be known in each extreme, beside—
(Or what means knowledge—to aspire or bide
Content with half-attaining? Hardly so!)
Made to know on, know ever, I must know
All to be known at any halting-stage
Of my soul's progress, such as earth, where wage
War, just for soul's instruction, pain with joy,
Folly with wisdom, all that works annoy
With all that quiets and contents,—in brief,
Good strives with evil.

                          "Now then for relief,
Friends, of your patience kindly curbed so long.
'What?' snarl you, 'is the fool's conceit thus strong—
Must the whole outside world in soul and sense
Suffer, that he grow sage at its expense?'
By no means! 'T is by merest touch of toe
I try—not trench on—ignorance, just know—
And so keep steady footing: how you fare,
Caught in the whirlpool—that 's the Cause's care,
Strong, wise, good,—this I know at any rate
In my own self,—but how may operate
With you—strength, wisdom, goodness—no least blink
Of knowledge breaks the darkness round me. Think!
Could I see plain, be somehow certified
All was illusion,—evil far and wide
Was good disguised,—why, out with one huge wipe
Goes knowledge from me. Type needs antitype:
As night needs day, as shine needs shade, so good
Needs evil: how were pity understood
Unless by pain? Make evident that pain
Permissibly masks pleasure—you abstain
From outstretch of the finger-tip that saves

A drowning fly. Who proffers help of hand
To weak Andromeda exposed on strand
At mercy of the monster? Were all true,
Help were not wanting: 'But 't is false,' cry you,
'Mere fancy-work of paint and brush!' No less,
Were mine the skill, the magic, to impress
Beholders with a confidence they saw
Life,—veritable flesh and blood in awe
Of just as true a sea-beast,—would they stare
Simply as now, or cry out, curse and swear,
Or call the gods to help, or catch up stick
And stone, according as their hearts were quick
Or sluggish? Well, some old artificer
Could do as much,—at least, so books aver,—
Able to make believe, while I, poor wight,
Make fancy, nothing more. Though wrong were right,
Could we but know—still wrong must needs seem wrong
To do right's service, prove men weak or strong,
Choosers of evil or of good. 'No such
Illusion possible!' Ah, friends, you touch
Just here my solid standing-place amid
The wash and welter, whence all doubts are bid
Back to the ledge they break against in foam,
Futility: my soul, and my soul's home
This body,—how each operates on each,
And how things outside, fact or feigning, teach
What good is and what evil,—just the same,
Be feigning or be fact the teacher,—blame
Diffidence nowise if, from this I judge
My point of vantage, not an inch I budge.
All—for myself—seems ordered wise and well
Inside it,—what reigns outside, who can tell?
Contrariwise, who needs be told 'The space
Which yields thee knowledge,—do its bounds embrace
Well-willing and wise-working, each at height?
Enongh: beyond thee lies the infinite—
Back to thy circumscription!'

"Back indeed!
Ending where I began—thus: retrocede,
Who will,—what comes first, take first, I advise!
Acquaint you with the body ere your eyes
Look upward: this Andromeda of mine—
Gaze on the beauty, Art hangs out for sign
There 's finer entertainment underneath.
Learn how they ministrate to life and death—
Those incommensurably marvellous
Contrivances which furnish forth the house

Where soul has sway! Though Master keep aloof,
Signs of his presence multiply from roof
To basement of the building. Look around,
Learn thoroughly,—no fear that you confound
Master with messuage! He 's away, no doubt,
But what if, all at once, you come upon
A startling proof—not that the Master gone
Was present lately—but that something—whence
Light comes—has pushed him into residence?
Was such the symbol's meaning,—old, uncouth—
That circle of the serpent, tail in mouth?
Only by looking low, ere looking high,
Comes penetration of the mystery."


XI


Thanks! After sermonizing, psalmody!
Now praise with pencil, Painter! Fools attaint
Your fame, forsooth, because its power inclines
To livelier colors, more attractive lines
Than suit some orthodox sad sickly saint
—Gray male emaciation, haply streaked
Carmine by scourgings—or they want, far worse—
Some self-scathed woman, framed to bless not curse
Nature that loved the form whereon hate wreaked
The wrongs you see. No, rather paint some full
Benignancy, the first and foremost boon
Of youth, health, strength,—show beauty's May, ere June
Undo the bud's blush, leave a rose to cull
—No poppy, neither! yet less perfect-pure,
Divinely-precious with life's dew besprent.
Show saintliness that's simply innocent
Of guessing sinnership exists to cure
All in good time! In time let age advance
And teach that knowledge helps—not ignorance—
The healing of the nations. Let my spark
Quicken your tinder! Burn with—Joan of Arc!
Not at the end, nor midway when there grew
The brave delusions, when rare fancies flew
Before the eyes, and in the ears of her
Strange voices woke imperiously astir:
No,—paint the peasant girl all peasant-like,
Spirit and flesh—the hour about to strike
When this should be transfigured, that inflamed,
By heart's admonishing "Thy country shamed,
Thy king shut out of all his realm except
One sorry corner!" and to life forth leapt

The indubitable lightning "Can there be
Country and king's salvation—all through me?"
Memorize that burst's moment, Francis! Tush—
None of the nonsense-writing! Fitlier brush
Shall clear off fancy's film-work and let show
Not what the foolish feign but the wise know—
Ask Sainte-Beuve else!—or better, Quicherat,
The downright-digger into truth that's—Bah,
Bettered by fiction? Well, of fact thus much
Concerns you, that "of prudishness no touch
From first to last defaced the maid; anon,
Camp-use compelling"—what says D'Alençon
Her fast friend?—"though I saw while she undressed
How fair she was—especially her breast—
Never had I a wild thought!"—as indeed
I nowise doubt. Much less would she take heed—
When eve came, and the lake, the hills around
Were all one solitude and silence,—found
Barriered impenetrably safe about,—
Take heed of interloping eyes shut out,
But quietly permit the air imbibe
Her naked beauty till ... but hear the scribe!
Now as she fain would bathe, one even-tide,
God's maid, this Joan, from the pool's edge she spied
The fair blue bird clowns call the Fisher-king:
And "'Las, sighed she, my Liege is such a thing
As thou, lord but of one poor lonely place
Out of his whole wide France: were mine the grace
To set my Dauphin free as thou, blue bird!"
Properly Martin-fisher—that's the word,
Not yours nor mine: folk said the rustic oath
In common use with her was—"By my troth"?
No,—"By my Martin"! Paint this! Only, turn
Her face away—that face about to burn
Into an angel's when the time is ripe!
That task's beyond you. Finished, Francis? Wipe
Pencil, scrape palette, and retire content!
"Omnia non omnibus"—no harm is meant!


WITH GERARD DE LAIRESSE

*The Art of Painting by Gerard le Lairesse, translated by J. F. Fritsch, was the "tome" to which Browning refers as having interested him when he was a boy and so given rise to this poem. The song at the end of the poem was first printed in a small volume called The New Amphion, published for the Edinburgh University Union Fancy Fair in 1886.*

I

Ah, but—because you were struck blind, could bless
Your sense no longer with the actual view
Of man and woman, those fair forms you drew
In happier days so duteously and true,—
Must I account my Gerard de Lairesse
All sorrow-smitten? He was hindered too
—Was this no hardship?—from producing, plain
To us who still have eyes, the pageantry
Which passed and passed before his busy brain
And, captured on his canvas, showed our sky
Traversed by flying shapes, earth stocked with brood
Of monsters,—centaurs bestial, satyrs lewd,—
Not without much Olympian glory, shapes
Of god and goddess in their gay escapes
From the severe serene: or haply paced
The antique ways, god-counselled, nymph-embraced,
Some early human kingly personage.
Such wonders of the teeming poet's-age
Were still to be: nay, these indeed began—
Are not the pictures extant?—till the ban
Of blindness struck both palette from his thumb
And pencil from his finger.


II

Blind—not dumb,
Else, Gerard, were my inmost bowels stirred
With pity beyond pity: no, the word
Was left upon your unmolested lips:
Your mouth unsealed, despite of eyes' eclipse,
Talked all brain's yearning into birth. I lack
Somehow the heart to wish your practice back
Which boasted hand's achievement in a score
Of veritable pictures, less or more,
Still to be seen: myself have seen them,—moved
To pay due homage to the man I loved
Because of that prodigious book he wrote
On Artistry's Ideal, by taking note,
Making acquaintance with his artist-work.
So my youth's piety obtained success
Of all too dubious sort: for, though it irk
To tell the issue, few or none would guess
From extant lines and colors, De Lairesse,
Your faculty, although each deftly-grouped
And aptly-ordered figure-piece was judged

Worthy a prince's purchase in its day.
Bearded experience bears not to be duped
Like boyish fancy: 'twas a boy that budged
No foot's breath from your visioned steps away
The while that memorable "Walk" he trudged
In your companionship,—the Book must say
Where, when and whither,—"Walk," come what come may,
No measurer of steps on this our globe
Shall ever match for marvels. Faustus' robe,
And Fortunatus' cap were gifts of price:
But—oh, your piece of sober sound advice
That artists should descry abundant worth
In trivial commonplace, nor groan at dearth
If fortune bade the painter's craft be plied
In vulgar town and country! Why despond
Because hemmed round by Dutch canals? Beyond
The ugly actual, lo, on every side
Imagination's limitless domain
Displayed a wealth of wondrous sounds and sights
Ripe to be realized by poet's brain
Acting on painter's brush! "Ye doubt? Poor wights,
What if I set example, go before,
While you come after, and we both explore
Holland turned Dreamland, taking care to note
Objects whereto my pupils may devote
Attention with advantage?"


III


So commenced
That "Walk" amid true wonders—none to you,
But huge to us ignobly common-sensed,
Purblind, while plain could proper optics view
In that old sepulchre by lightning split,
Whereof the lid bore carven,—any dolt
Imagines why,—Jove's very thunderbolt:
You who could straight perceive, by glance at it,
This tomb must needs be Phaeton's! In a trice,
Confirming that conjecture, close on hand,
Behold, half out, half in the ploughed-up sand,
A chariot-wheel explained its bolt-device:
What other than the Chariot of the Sun
Ever let drop the like? Consult the tome—
I bid inglorious tarriers-at-home—
For greater still surprise the while that "Walk"
Went on and on, to end as it begun,
Chokefull of chances, changes, every one

No whit less wondrous. What was there to balk
Us, who had eyes, from seeing? You with none
Missed not a marvel: wherefore? Let us talk.


IV


Say am I right? Your sealed sense moved your mind,
Free from obstruction, to compassionate
Art's power left powerless, and supply the blind
With fancies worth all facts denied by fate.
Mind could invent things, add to—take away,
At pleasure, leave out trifles mean and base
Which vex the sight that cannot say them nay
But, where mind plays the master, have no place.
And bent on banishing was mind, be sure,
All except beauty from its mustered tribe
Of objects apparitional which lure
Painter to show and poet to describe—
That imagery of the antique song
Truer than truth's self. Fancy's rainbow-birth
Conceived 'mid clouds in Greece, could glance along
Your passage o'er Dutch veritable earth,
As with ourselves, who see, familiar throng
About our pacings men and women worth
Nowise a glance—so poets apprehend—
Since naught avails portraying them in verse:
While painters turn upon the heel, intend
To spare their work the critic's ready curse
Due to the daily and undignified.


V


I who myself contentedly abide
Awake, nor want the wings of dream,—who tramp
Earth's common surface, rough, smooth, dry or damp,
—I understand alternatives, no less
Conceive your soul's leap, Gerard de Lairesse!
How were it could I mingle false with true,
Boast, with the sights I see, your vision too?
Advantage would it prove or detriment
If I saw double? Could I gaze intent
On Dryope plucking the blossoms red,
As you, whereat her lote-tree writhed and bled!
Yet lose no gain, no hard fast wide-awake
Having and holding nature for the sake
Of nature only—nymph and lote-tree thus

Gained by the loss of fruit not fabulous,
Apple of English homesteads, where I see
Nor seek more than crisp buds a struggling bee
Uncrumples, caught by sweet he clambers through?
Truly, a moot point: make it plain to me,
Who, bee-like, sate sense with the simply true,
Nor seek to heighten that sufficiency
By help of feignings proper to the page—
Earth's surface-blank whereon the elder age
Put color, poetizing—poured rich life
On what were else a dead ground—nothingness—
Until the solitary world grew rife
With Joves and Junos, nymphs and satyrs. Yes,
The reason was, fancy composed the strife
'Twixt sense and soul: for sense, my De Lairesse,
Cannot content itself with outward things,
Mere beauty: soul must needs know whence there springs—
How, when and why—what sense but loves, nor lists
To know at all.


VI


Not one of man's acquists
Ought he resignedly to lose, methinks:
So, point me out which was it of the links
Snapt first, from out the chain which used to bind
Our earth to heaven, and yet for you, since blind,
Subsisted still efficient and intact?
Oh, we can fancy too! but somehow fact
Has got to—say, not so much push aside
Fancy, as to declare its place supplied
By fact unseen but no less fact the same,
Which mind bids sense accept. Is mind to blame,
Or sense,—does that usurp, this abdicate?
First of all, as you "walked"—were it too late
For us to walk, if so we willed? Confess
We have the sober feet still, De Lairesse!
Why not the freakish brain too, that must needs
Supplement nature—not see flowers and weeds
Simply as such, but link with each and all
The ultimate perfection—what we call
Rightly enough the human shape divine?
The rose? No rose unless it disentwine
From Venus' wreath the while she bends to kiss
Her deathly love?

VII

Plain retrogression, this!
No, no: we poets go not back at all:
What you did we could do—from great to small
Sinking assuredly: if this world last
One moment longer when Man finds its Past
Exceed its Present—blame the Protoplast!
If we no longer see as you of old,
'Tis we see deeper. Progress for the bold!
You saw the body, 'tis the soul we see.
Try now! Bear witness while you walk with me,
I see as you: if we loose arms, stop pace,
'Tis that you stand still, I conclude the race
Without your company. Come, walk once more
The "Walk:" if I to-day as you of yore
See just like you the blind—then sight shall cry
—The whole long day quite gone through—victory!


VIII

Thunders on thunders, doubling and redoubling
Doom o'er the mountain, while a sharp white fire
Now shone, now sheared its rusty herbage, troubling
Hardly the fir-boles, now discharged its ire
Full where some pine-tree's solitary spire
Crashed down, defiant to the last: till—lo,
The motive of the malice!—all aglow,
Circled with flame there yawned a sudden rift
I' the rock-face, and I saw a form erect
Front and defy the outrage, while—as checked,
Chidden, beside him dauntless in the drift—
Cowered a heaped creature, wing and wing outspread
In deprecation o'er the crouching head
Still hungry for the feast foregone awhile.
O thou, of scorn's unconquerable smile,
Was it when this—Jove's feathered fury—slipped
Gore-glutted from the heart's core whence he ripped—
This eagle-hound—neither reproach nor prayer—
Baffled, in one more fierce attempt to tear
Fate's secret from thy safeguard,—was it then
That all these thunders rent earth, ruined air
To reach thee, pay thy patronage of men?
He thundered,—to withdraw, as beast to lair,
Before the triumph on thy pallid brow.
Gather the night again about thee now,
Hate on, love ever! Morn is breaking there—

The granite ridge pricks through the mist, turns gold
As wrong turns right. O laughters manifold
Of ocean's ripple at dull earth's despair!


IX

But morning's laugh sets all the crags alight
Above the baffled tempest: tree and tree
Stir themselves from the stupor of the night,
And every strangled branch resumes its right
To breathe, shakes loose dark's clinging dregs, waves free
In dripping glory. Prone the runnels plunge,
While earth, distent with moisture like a sponge,
Smokes up, and leaves each plant its gem to see,
Each grass-blade's glory-glitter. Had I known
The torrent now turned river?—masterful
Making its rush o'er tumbled ravage—stone
And stub which barred the froths and foams: no bull
Ever broke bounds in formidable sport
More overwhelmingly, till lo, the spasm
Sets him to dare that last mad leap: report
Who may—his fortunes in the deathly chasm
That swallows him in silence! Rather turn
Whither, upon the upland, pedestalled
Into the broad day-splendor, whom discern
These eyes but thee, supreme one, rightly called
Moon-maid in heaven above and, here below,
Earth's huntress-queen? I note the garb succinct
Saving from smirch that purity of snow
From breast to knee—snow's self with just the tinct
Of the apple-blossom's heart-blush. Ah, the bow
Slack-strung her fingers grasp, where, ivory-linked
Horn curving blends with horn, a moonlike pair
Which mimic the brow's crescent sparkling so—
As if a star's live restless fragment winked
Proud yet repugnant, captive in such hair!
What hope along the hillside, what far bliss
Lets the crisp hair-plaits fall so low they kiss
Those lucid shoulders? Must a morn so blithe
Needs have its sorrow when the twang and hiss
Tell that from out thy sheaf one shaft makes writhe
Its victim, thou unerring Artemis?
Why did the chamois stand so fair a mark
Arrested by the novel shape he dreamed
Was bred of liquid marble in the dark
Depths of the mountain's womb which ever teemed
With novel births of wonder? Not one spark

Of pity in that steel-gray glance which gleamed
At the poor hoof's protesting as it stamped
Idly the granite? Let me glide unseen
From thy proud presence: well mayst thou be queen
Of all those strange and sudden deaths which damped
So oft Love's torch and Hymen's taper lit
For happy marriage till the maidens paled
And perished on the temple-step, assailed
By—what except to envy must man's wit
Impute that sure implacable release
Of life from warmth and joy? But death means peace.


X

Noon is the conqueror,—not a spray, nor leaf,
Nor herb, nor blossom but has rendered up
Its morning dew: the valley seemed one cup
Of cloud-smoke, but the vapor's reign was brief;
Sun-smitten, see, it hangs—the filmy haze—
Gray-garmenting the herbless mountain-side,
To soothe the day's sharp glare: while far and wide
Above unclouded burns the sky, one blaze
With fierce immitigable blue, no bird
Ventures to spot by passage. E'en of peaks
Which still presume there, plain each pale point speaks
In wan transparency of waste incurred
By over-daring: far from me be such!
Deep in the hollow, rather, where combine
Tree, shrub and brier to roof with shade and cool
The remnant of some lily-strangled pool,
Edged round with mossy fringing soft and fine.
Smooth lie the bottom slabs, and overhead
Watch elder, bramble, rose, and service-tree
And one beneficent rich barberry
Jewelled all over with fruit-pendants red.
What have I seen! O Satyr, well I know
How sad thy case, and what a world of woe
Was hid by the brown visage furry-framed
Only for mirth: who otherwise could think—
Marking thy mouth gape still on laughter's brink,
Thine eyes a-swim with merriment unnamed
But haply guessed at by their furtive wink?
And all the while a heart was panting sick
Behind that shaggy bulwark of thy breast—
Passion it was that made those breath-bursts thick
I took for mirth, subsiding into rest.
So, it was Lyda—she of all the train

Of forest-thridding nymphs,—'twas only she
Turned from thy rustic homage in disdain,
Saw but that poor uncouth outside of thee,
And, from her circling sisters, mocked a pain
Echo had pitied—whom Pan loved in vain—
For she was wishful to partake thy glee,
Mimic thy mirth—who loved her not again,
Savage for Lyda's sake. She crouches there—
Thy cruel beauty, slumberously laid
Supine on heaped-up beast-skins, unaware
Thy steps have traced her to the briery glade,
Thy greedy hands disclose the cradling lair,
Thy hot eyes reach and revel on the maid!


XI


Now, what should this be for? The sun's decline
Seems as he lingered lest he lose some act
Dread and decisive, some prodigious fact
Like thunder from the safe sky's sapphirine
About to alter earth's conditions, packed
With fate for nature's self that waits, aware
What mischief unsuspected in the air
Menaces momently a cataract.
Therefore it is that yonder space extends
Untrenched upon by any vagrant tree,
Shrub, weed well-nigh; they keep their bounds, leave free
The platform for what actors? Foes or friends,
Here come they trooping silent: heaven suspends
Purpose the while they range themselves. I see!
Bent on a battle, two vast powers agree
This present and no after-contest ends
One or the other's grasp at rule in reach
Over the race of man—host fronting host,
As statue statue fronts—wrath-molten each,
Solidified by hate,—earth halved almost,
To close once more in chaos. Yet two shapes
Show prominent, each from the universe
Of minions round about him, that disperse
Like cloud-obstruction when a bolt escapes.
Who flames first? Macedonian, is it thou?
Ay, and who fronts thee, King Darius, drapes
His form with purple, fillet-folds his brow.


XII

What, then the long day dies at last? Abrupt
The sun that seemed, in stooping, sure to melt
Our mountain-ridge, is mastered: black the belt
Of westward crags, his gold could not corrupt,
Barriers again the valley, lets the flow
Of lavish glory waste itself away
—Whither? For new climes, fresh eyes breaks the day!
Night was not to be baffled. If the glow
Were all that's gone from us! Did clouds, afloat
So filmily but now, discard no rose,
Sombre throughout the fleeciness that grows
A sullen uniformity. I note
Rather displeasure,—in the overspread
Change from the swim of gold to one pale lead
Oppressive to malevolence,—than late
Those amorous yearnings when the aggregate
Of cloudlets pressed that each and all might sate
Its passion and partake in relics red
Of day's bequeathment: now, a frown instead
Estranges, and affrights who needs must fare
On and on till his journey ends: but where?
Caucasus? Lost now in the night. Away
And far enough lies that Arcadia.
The human heroes tread the world's dark way
No longer. Yet I dimly see almost—
Yes, for my last adventure! 'Tis a ghost.
So drops away the beauty! There he stands
Voiceless, scarce strives with deprecating hands ...


XIII


Enough! Stop further fooling, De Lairesse!
My fault, not yours! Some fitter way express
Heart's satisfaction that the Past indeed
Is past, gives way before Life's best and last,
The all-including Future! What were life
Did soul stand still therein, forego her strife
Through the ambiguous Present to the goal
Of some all-reconciling Future? Soul,
Nothing has been which shall not bettered be
Hereafter,—leave the root, by law's decree
Whence springs the ultimate and perfect tree!
Busy thee with unearthing root? Nay, climb—
Quit trunk, branch, leaf and flower—reach, rest sublime
Where fruitage ripens in the blaze of day!
O'erlook, despise, forget, throw flower away,
Intent on progress? No whit more than stop

Ascent therewith to dally, screen the top
Sufficiency of yield by interposed
Twistwork bold foot gets free from. Wherefore glozed
The poets—"Dream afresh old godlike shapes,
Recapture ancient fable that escapes,
Push back reality, repeople earth
With vanished falseness, recognize no worth
In fact new-born unless 't is rendered back
Pallid by fancy, as the western rack
Of fading cloud bequeaths the lake some gleam
Of its gone glory!"

## XIV

Let things be—not seem,
I counsel rather,—do, and nowise dream!
Earth's young significance is all to learn:
The dead Greek lore lies buried in the urn
Where who seeks fire finds ashes. Ghost, forsooth!
What was the best Greece babbled of as truth?
"A shade, a wretched nothing,—sad, thin, drear,
Cold, dark, it holds on to the lost loves here,
If hand have haply sprinkled o'er the dead
Three charitable dust-heaps, made mouth red
One moment by the sip of sacrifice:
Just so much comfort thaws the stubborn ice
Slow-thickening upward till it choke at length
The last faint flutter craving—not for strength,
Not beauty, not the riches and the rule
O'er men that made life life indeed." Sad school
Was Hades! Gladly,—might the dead but slink
To life back,—to the dregs once more would drink
Each interloper, drain the humblest cup
Fate mixes for humanity.

## XV

Cheer up,—
Be death with me, as with Achilles erst,
Of Man's calamities the last and worst:
Take it so! By proved potency that still
Makes perfect, be assured, come what come will,
What once lives never dies—what here attains
To a beginning, has no end, still gains
And never loses aught: when, where, and how—
Lies in Law's lap. What 's death then? Even now

With so much knowledge is it hard to bear
Brief interposing ignorance? Is care
For a creation found at fault just there—
There where the heart breaks bond and outruns time,
To reach not follow what shall be?


XVI


Here 's rhyme
Such as one makes now,—say, when Spring repeats
That miracle the Greek Bard sadly greets:
"Spring for the tree and herb—no Spring for us!"
Let Spring come: why, a man salutes her thus:

Dance, yellows and whites and reds,—
Lead your gay orgy, leaves, stalks, heads
Astir with the wind in the tulip-beds!

There 's sunshine; scarcely a wind at all
Disturbs starved grass and daisies small
On a certain mound by a churchyard wall.

Daisies and grass be my heart's bedfellows
On the mound wind spares and sunshine mellows:
Dance you, reds and whites and yellows!


WITH CHARLES AVISON

*The manuscript of the Grand March written by Avison was in the possession of Browning's father, and a copy is given at the end of the poem. The Relfe who is two or three times mentioned was Browning's teacher of music, who was a learned contrapuntist.*

I

How strange!—but, first of all, the little fact
Which led my fancy forth. This bitter morn
Showed me no object in the stretch forlorn
Of garden-ground beneath my window, backed
By yon worn wall wherefrom the creeper, tacked
To clothe its brickwork, hangs now, rent and racked
By five months' cruel winter,—showed no torn
And tattered ravage worse for eyes to see
Than just one ugly space of clearance, left
Bare even of the bones which used to be
Warm wrappage, safe embracement: this one cleft—

—Oh, what a life and beauty filled it up
Startlingly, when methought the rude clay cup
Ran over with poured bright wine! 'T was a bird
Breast-deep there, tugging at his prize, deterred
No whit by the fast-falling snow-flake: gain
Such prize my blackcap must by might and main—
The cloth-shred, still a-flutter from its nail
That fixed a spray once. Now, what told the tale
To thee,—no townsman but born orchard-thief,—
That here—surpassing moss-tuft, beard from sheaf
Of sun-scorched barley, horsehairs long and stout,
All proper country-pillage—here, no doubt,
Was just the scrap to steal should line thy nest
Superbly? Off he flew, his bill possessed
The booty sure to set his wife's each wing
Greenly a-quiver. How they climb and cling,
Hang parrot-wise to bough, these blackcaps! Strange
Seemed to a city-dweller that the finch
Should stray so far to forage: at a pinch,
Was not the fine wool's self within his range
—Filchings on every fence? But no: the need
Was of this rag of manufacture, spoiled
By art, and yet by nature near unsoiled,
New-suited to what scheming finch would breed
In comfort, this uncomfortable March.


II


Yet—by the first pink blossom on the larch!—
This was scarce stranger than that memory,—
In want of what should cheer the stay-at-home,
My soul,—must straight clap pinion, well-nigh roam
A century back, nor once close plume, descry
The appropriate rag to plunder, till she pounced—
Pray, on what relic of a brain long still?
What old-world work proved forage for the bill
Of memory the far-flyer? "March" announced,
I verily believe, the dead and gone
Name of a music-maker: one of such
In England as did little or did much,
But, doing, had their day once. Avison!
Singly and solely for an air of thine,
Bold-stepping "March," foot stept to ere my hand
Could stretch an octave, I o'erlooked the band
Of majesties familiar, to decline
On thee—not too conspicuous on the list
Of worthies who by help of pipe or wire

Expressed in sound rough rage or soft desire—
Thou, whilom of Newcastle organist!


III

So much could one—well, thinnish air effect!
Am I ungrateful? for, your March, styled "Grand,"
Did veritably seem to grow, expand,
And greaten up to title as, unchecked,
Dream-marchers marched, kept marching, slow and sure,
In time, to tune, unchangeably the same,
From nowhere into nowhere,—out they came,
Onward they passed, and in they went. No lure
Of novel modulation pricked the flat
Forthright persisting melody,—no hint
That discord, sound asleep beneath the flint,
Struck—might spring spark-like, claim due tit-for-tat,
Quenched in a concord. No! Yet, such the might
Of quietude's immutability,
That somehow coldness gathered warmth, well-nigh
Quickened—which could not be!—grew burning-bright
With fife-shriek, cymbal-clash and trumpet-blare,
To drum-accentuation: pacing turned
Striding, and striding grew gigantic, spurned
At last the narrow space 'twixt earth and air,
So shook me back into my sober self.


IV

And where woke I? The March had set me down
There whence I plucked the measure, as his brown
Frayed flannel-bit my blackcap. Great John Relfe,
Master of mine, learned, redoubtable,
It little needed thy consummate skill
To fitly figure such a bass! The key
Was—should not memory play me false—well, C.
Ay, with the Greater Third, in Triple Time,
Three crochets to a bar: no change, I grant,
Except from Tonic down to Dominant.
And yet—and yet—if I could put in rhyme
The manner of that marching!—which had stopped
—I wonder, where?—but that my weak self dropped
From out the ranks, to rub eyes disentranced
And feel that, after all the way advanced,
Back must I foot it, I and my compeers,
Only to reach, across a hundred years,

The bandsman Avison whose little book
And large tune thus had led me the long way
(As late a rag my blackcap) from to-day
And to-day's music-manufacture,—Brahms,
Wagner, Dvorak, Liszt,—to where—trumpets, shawms,
Show yourselves joyful!—Handel reigns—supreme?
By no means! Buononcini's work is theme
For fit laudation of the impartial few:
(We stand in England, mind you!) Fashion too
Favors Geminiani—of those choice
Concertos: nor there wants a certain voice
Raised in thy favor likewise, famed Pepusch
Dear to our great-grandfathers! In a bush
Of Doctor's wig, they prized thee timing beats
While Greenway trilled "Alexis." Such were feats
Of music in thy day—dispute who list—
Avison, of Newcastle organist!


V


And here 's your music all alive once more—
As once it was alive, at least: just so
The figured worthies of a waxwork-show
Attest—such people, years and years ago,
Looked thus when outside death had life below,
—Could say "We are now" not "We were of yore,"
—"Feel how our pulses leap!" and not "Explore—
Explain why quietude has settled o'er
Surface once all awork!" Ay, such a "Suite"
Roused heart to rapture, such a "Fugue" would catch
Soul heavenwards up, when time was: why attach
Blame to exhausted faultlessness, no match
For fresh achievement? Feat once—ever feat!
How can completion grow still more complete?
Hear Avison! He tenders evidence
That music in his day as much absorbed
Heart and soul then as Wagner's music now,
Perfect from centre to circumference—
Orbed to the full can be but fully orbed:
And yet—and yet—whence comes it that "O Thou"—
Sighed by the soul at eve to Hesperus—
Will not again take wing and fly away
(Since fatal Wagner fixed it fast for us)
In some unmodulated minor? Nay,
Even by Handel's help!

VI

I state it thus:
There is no truer truth obtainable
By Man than comes of music. "Soul"—(accept
A word which vaguely names what no adept
In word-use fits and fixes so that still
Thing shall not slip word's fetter and remain
Innominate as first, yet, free again,
Is no less recognized the absolute
Fact underlying that same other fact
Concerning which no cavil can dispute
Our nomenclature when we call it "Mind"—
Something not Matter)—"Soul," who seeks shall find
Distinct beneath that something. You exact
An illustrative image? This may suit.


VII

We see a work: the worker works behind,
Invisible himself. Suppose his act
Be to o'erarch a gulf: he digs, transports,
Shapes and, through enginery—all sizes, sorts,
Lays stone by stone until a floor compact
Proves our bridged causeway. So works Mind—by stress
Of faculty, with loose facts, more or less,
Builds up our solid knowledge: all the same,
Underneath rolls what Mind may hide not tame,
An element which works beyond our guess,
Soul, the unsounded sea—whose lift of surge,
Spite of all superstructure, lets emerge,
In flower and foam, Feeling from out the deeps
Mind arrogates no mastery upon—
Distinct indisputably. Has there gone
To dig up, drag forth, render smooth from rough
Mind's flooring,—operosity enough?
Still the successive labor of each inch,
Who lists may learn: from the last turn of winch
That let the polished slab-stone find its place,
To the first prod of pickaxe at the base
Of the unquarried mountain,—what was all
Mind's varied process except natural,
Nay, easy even, to descry, describe,
After our fashion? "So worked Mind: its tribe
Of senses ministrant above, below,
Far, near, or now or haply long ago
Brought to pass knowledge." But Soul's sea,—drawn whence,

Fed how, forced whither,—by what evidence
Of ebb and flow, that 's felt beneath the tread,
Soul has its course 'neath Mind's work overhead,—
Who tells of, tracks to source the founts of Soul?
Yet wherefore heaving sway and restless roll
This side and that, except to emulate
Stability above? To match and mate
Feeling with knowledge,—make as manifest
Soul's work as Mind's work, turbulence as rest,
Hates, loves, joys, woes, hopes, fears, that rise and sink
Ceaselessly, passion's transient flit and wink,
A ripple's tinting or a spume-sheet's spread
Whitening the wave,—to strike all this life dead,
Run mercury into a mould like lead,
And henceforth have the plain result to show—
How we Feel, hard and fast as what we Know—
This were the prize and is the puzzle!—which
Music essays to solve: and here 's the hitch
That balks her of full triumph else to boast.


VIII

All Arts endeavor this, and she the most
Attains thereto, yet fails of touching: why?
Does Mind get Knowledge from Art's ministry?
What 's known once is known ever: Arts arrange,
Dissociate, re-distribute, interchange
Part with part, lengthen, broaden, high or deep
Construct their bravest,—still such pains produce
Change, not creation: simply what lay loose
At first lies firmly after, what design
Was faintly traced in hesitating line
Once on a time, grows firmly resolute
Henceforth and evermore. Now, could we shoot
Liquidity into a mould,—some way
Arrest Soul's evanescent moods, and keep
Unalterably still the forms that leap
To life for once by help of Art!—which yearns
To save its capture: Poetry discerns,
Painting is 'ware of passion's rise and fall,
Bursting, subsidence, intermixture—all
A-seethe within the gulf. Each Art a-strain
Would stay the apparition,—nor in vain:
The Poet's word-mesh, Painter's sure and swift
Color-and-line-throw—proud the prize they lift!
Thus felt Man and thus looked Man,—passions caught
I' the midway swim of sea,—not much, if aught,

Of nether-brooding loves, hates, hopes and fears,
Enwombed past Art's disclosure. Fleet the years,
And still the Poet's page holds Helena
At gaze from topmost Troy—"But where are they,
My brothers, in the armament I name
Hero by hero? Can it be that shame
For their lost sister holds them from the war?"
—Knowing not they already slept afar
Each of them in his own dear native land.
Still on the Painter's fresco, from the hand
Of God takes Eve the life-spark whereunto
She trembles up from nothingness. Outdo
Both of them, Music! Dredging deeper yet,
Drag into day,—by sound, thy master-net,—
The abysmal bottom-growth, ambiguous thing
Unbroken of a branch, palpitating
With limbs' play and life's semblance! There it lies.
Marvel and mystery, of mysteries
And marvels, most to love and laud thee for!
Save it from chance and change we most abhor!
Give momentary feeling permanence,
So that thy capture hold, a century hence,
Truth's very heart of truth as, safe to-day,
The Painter's Eve, the Poet's Helena
Still rapturously bend, afar still throw
The wistful gaze! Thanks, Homer, Angelo!
Could Music rescue thus from Soul's profound,
Give feeling immortality by sound,
Then were she queenliest of Arts! Alas—
As well expect the rainbow not to pass!
"Praise 'Radamisto'—love attains therein
To perfect utterance! Pity—what shall win
Thy secret like 'Rinaldo'?"—so men said:
Once all was perfume—now, the flower is dead—
They spied tints, sparks have left the spar! Love, hate,
Joy, fear, survive,—alike importunate
As ever to go walk the world again,
Nor ghost-like pant for outlet all in vain
Till Music loose them, fit each filmily
With form enough to know and name it by
For any recognizer sure of ken
And sharp of ear, no grosser denizen
Of earth than needs be. Nor to such appeal
Is Music long obdurate: off they steal—
How gently, dawn-doomed phantoms! back come they
Full-blooded with new crimson of broad day—
Passion made palpable once more. Ye look
Your last on Handel? Gaze your first on Gluck!

Why wistful search, O waning ones, the chart
Of stars for you while Haydn, while Mozart
Occupies heaven? These also, fanned to fire,
Flamboyant wholly,—so perfections tire,—
Whiten to wanness, till ... let others note
The ever-new invasion!


IX

I devote
Rather my modicum of parts to use
What power may yet avail to re-infuse
(In fancy, please you!) sleep that looks like death
With momentary liveliness, lend breath
To make the torpor half inhale. O Relfe,
An all-unworthy pupil, from the shelf
Of thy laboratory, dares unstop
Bottle, ope box, extract thence pinch and drop
Of dusts and dews a many thou didst shrine
Each in its right receptacle, assign
To each its proper office, letter large
Label and label, then with solemn charge,
Reviewing learnedly the list complete
Of chemical reactives, from thy feet
Push down the same to me, attent below,
Power in abundance: armed wherewith I go
To play the enlivener. Bring good antique stuff!
Was it alight once? Still lives spark enough
For breath to quicken, run the smouldering ash
Red right-through. What, "stone-dead" were fools so rash
As style my Avison, because he lacked
Modern appliance, spread out phrase unracked
By modulations fit to make each hair
Stiffen upon his wig? See there—and there!
I sprinkle my reactives, pitch broadcast
Discords and resolutions, turn aghast
Melody's easy-going, jostle law
With license, modulate (no Bach in awe)
Change enharmonically (Hudl to thank)
And lo, upstart the flamelets,—what was blank
Turns scarlet, purple, crimson! Straightway scanned
By eyes that like new lustre—Love once more
Yearns through the Largo, Hatred as before
Rages in the Rubato: e'en thy March,
My Avison, which, sooth to say—(ne'er arch
Eyebrows in anger!)—timed, in Georgian years
The step precise of British Grenadiers

To such a nicety,—if score I crowd,
If rhythm I break, if beats I vary,—tap
At bar's off-starting turns true thunder-clap,
Eyer the pace augmented till—what 's here?
Titanic striding toward Olympus!


X

Fear
No such irreverent innovation! Still
Glide on, go rolling, water-like, at will—
Nay, were thy melody in monotone,
The due three-parts dispensed with!


XI

This alone
Comes of my tiresome talking: Music's throne
Seats somebody whom somebody unseats,
And whom in turn—by who knows what new feats
Of strength—shall somebody as sure push down,
Consign him dispossessed of sceptre, crown,
And orb imperial—whereto? Never dream
That what once lived shall ever die! They seem
Dead—do they? lapsed things lost in limbo? Bring
Our life to kindle theirs, and straight each king
Starts, you shall see, stands up, from head to foot
No inch that is not Purcell! Wherefore? (Suit
Measure to subject, first—no marching on
Yet in thy bold C major, Avison,
As suited step a minute since: no: wait—
Into the minor key first modulate—
Gently with A, now—in the Lesser Third!)


XII

Of all the lamentable debts incurred
By Man through buying knowledge, this were worst:
That he should find his last gain prove his first
Was futile—merely nescience absolute,
Not knowledge in the bud which holds a fruit
Haply undreamed of in the soul's Spring-tide,
Pursed in the petals Summer opens wide,
And Autumn, withering, rounds to perfect ripe,—
Not this,—but ignorance, a blur to wipe

From human records, late it graced so much.
"Truth—this attainment? Ah, but such and such
Beliefs of yore seemed inexpugnable
When we attained them! E'en as they, so will
This their successor have the due morn, noon,
Evening and night—just as an old-world tune
Wears out and drops away, until who hears
Smilingly questions—'This it was brought tears
Once to all eyes,—this roused heart's rapture once?'
So will it be with truth that, for the nonce,
Styles itself truth perennial: 'ware its wile!
Knowledge turns nescience,—foremost on the file,
Simply proves first of our delusions."


XIII


Now—
Blare it forth, bold C major! Lift thy brow,
Man, the immortal, that wast never fooled
With gifts no gifts at all, nor ridiculed—
Man knowing—he who nothing knew! As Hope,
Fear, Joy, and Grief,—though ampler stretch and scope
They seek and find in novel rhythm, fresh phrase,—
Were equally existent in far days
Of Music's dim beginning—even so,
Truth was at full within thee long ago,
Alive as now it takes what latest shape
May startle thee by strangeness. Truths escape
Time's insufficient garniture: they fade,
They fall—those sheathings now grown sere, whose aid
Was infinite to truth they wrapped, saved fine
And free through March frost: May dews crystalline
Nourish truth merely,—does June boast the fruit
As—not new vesture merely but, to boot,
Novel creation? Soon shall fade and fall
Myth after myth—the husk-like lies I call
New truth's corolla-safeguard: Autumn comes,
So much the better!


XIV


Therefore—bang the drums,
Blow the trumpets, Avison! March-motive? that's
Truth which endures resetting. Sharps and flats,
Lavish at need, shall dance athwart thy score
When ophicleide and bombardon's uproar

Mate the approaching trample, even now
Big in the distance—or my ears deceive—
Of federated England, fitly weave
March-music for the Future!


XV


Or suppose
Back, and not forward, transformation goes?
Once more some sable-stoled procession—say,
From Little-ease to Tyburn—wends its way,
Out of the dungeon to the gallows-tree
Where heading, hacking, hanging is to be
Of half-a-dozen recusants—this day
Three hundred years ago! How duly drones
Elizabethan plain-song—dim antique
Grown clarion-clear the while I humbly wreak
A classic vengeance on thy March! It moans—
Larges and Longs and Breves displacing quite
Crotchet-and-quaver pertness—brushing bars
Aside and filling vacant sky with stars
Hidden till now that day return to night.


XVI


Nor night nor day: one purpose move us both,
Be thy mood mine! As thou wast minded, Man 's
The cause our music champions: I were loth
To think we cheered our troop to Preston Pans
Ignobly: back to times of England's best!
Parliament stands for privilege—life and limb
Guards Hollis, Haselrig, Strode, Hampden, Pym,
The famous Five. There 's rumor of arrest.
Bring up the Train Bands, Southwark! They protest:
Shall we not all join chorus? Hark the hymn,
—Rough, rude, robustious—homely heart a-throb,
Harsh voice a-hallo, as beseems the mob!
How good is noise! what 's silence but despair
Of making sound match gladness never there?
Give me some great glad "subject," glorious Bach,
Where cannon-roar not organ-peal we lack!
Join in, give voice robustious rude and rough,—
Avison helps—so heart lend noise enough!

Fife, trump, drum, sound! and singers then
Marching say "Pym, the man of men!"

Up, heads, your proudest,—out throats, your loudest—
"Somerset's Pym!"

Strafford from the block, Eliot from the den,
Foes, friends, shout "Pym, our citizen!"
Wail, the foes he quelled,—hail, the friends he held,
"Tavistock's Pym!"

Hearts prompt heads, hands that ply the pen
Teach babes unborn the where and when.
—Tyrants, he braved them,—patriots, he saved them—
"Westminster's Pym!"

[Music]

**Inside the House of Fust, Mayence, 1457.**

**FIRST FRIEND**
Up, up, up—next step of the staircase
Lands us, lo, at the chamber of dread!

**SECOND FRIEND**
Locked and barred?

**THIRD FRIEND**
Door open—the rare case!

**FOURTH FRIEND**
Ay, there he leans—lost wretch!

**FIFTH FRIEND**
His head
Sunk on his desk 'twixt his arms outspread!

\*   \*   \*   \*   \*

**SIXTH FRIEND**
Hallo,—wake, man, ere God thunderstrike Mayence
—Mulct for thy sake who art Satan's, John Fust!
Satan installed here, God's rule in abeyance,
Mayence some morning may crumble to dust.
Answer our questions thou shalt and thou must!

**SEVENTH FRIEND**

Softly and fairly! Wherefore a-gloom?
Greet us, thy gossipry, cousin and sib!
Raise the forlorn brow, Fust! Make room—
Let daylight through arms which, enfolding thee, crib
From those clenched lids the comfort of sunshine!

**FIRST FRIEND**

So glib

Thy tongue slides to "comfort" already? Not mine!
Behoove us deal roundly: the wretch is distraught
—Too well I guess wherefore! Behooves a Divine
—Such as I, by grace, boast me—to threaten one caught
In the enemy's toils,—setting "comfort" at naught.

**SECOND FRIEND**

Nay, Brother, so hasty? I heard—nor long since—
Of a certain Black Art'sman who,—helplessly bound
By rash pact with Satan,—through paying—why mince
The matter?—fit price to the Church,—safe and sound
Full a year after death in his grave-clothes was found.

Whereas 't is notorious the Fiend claims his due
During lifetime,—comes clawing, with talons aflame,
The soul from the flesh-rags left smoking and blue:
So it happed with John Faust; lest John Fust fare the same,—
Look up, I adjure thee by God's holy name!

For neighbors and friends—no foul hell-brood flock we!
Saith Solomon "Words of the wise are as goads:"
Ours prick but to startle from torpor, set free
Soul and sense from death's drowse!

**FIRST FRIEND**

And soul, wakened, unloads
Much sin by confession: no mere palinodes!

—"I was youthful and wanton, am old yet no sage:
When angry I cursed, struck and slew: did I want?
Right and left did I rob: though no war I dared wage
With the Church (God forbid!)—harm her least ministrant—
Still I outraged all else. Now that strength is grown scant,

"I am probity's self"—no such bleatings as these!
But avowal of guilt so enormous, it balks
Tongue's telling. Yet penitence prompt may appease

God's wrath at thy bond with the Devil who stalks
—Strides hither to strangle thee!

**FUST**
Childhood so talks.—

Not rare wit nor ripe age—ye boast them, my neighbors!—
Should lay such a charge on your townsman, this Fust
Who, known for a life spent in pleasures and labors
If freakish yet venial, could scarce be induced
To traffic with fiends.

**FIRST FRIEND**
So, my words have unloosed

A plie from those pale lips corrugate but now?

**FUST**
Lost count me, yet not as ye lean to surmise.

**FIRST FRIEND**
To surmise? to establish! Unbury that brow!
Look up, that thy judge may read clear in thine eyes!

**SECOND FRIEND**
By your leave, Brother Barnabite! Mine to advise!

—Who arraign thee, John Fust! What was bruited erewhile
Now bellows through Mayence. All cry—thou hast trucked
Salvation away for lust's solace! Thy smile
Takes its hue from hell's smoulder!

**FUST**
Too certain! I sucked
—Got drunk at the nipple of sense.

**SECOND FRIEND**
Thou hast ducked—

Art drowned there, say rather! Faugh—fleshly disport!
How else but by help of Sir Belial didst win
That Venus-like lady, no drudge of thy sort
Could lure to become his accomplice in sin?
Folk nicknamed her Helen of Troy!

**FIRST FRIEND**
Best begin

At the very beginning. Thy father,—all knew,
A mere goldsmith ...

**FUST**
Who knew him, perchance may know this—
He dying left much gold and jewels no few:
Whom these help to court with, but seldom shall miss
The love of a leman: true witchcraft, I wis!

\*     \*     \*     \*     \*

**FIRST FRIEND**
Dost flout me? 'T is said, in debauchery's guild
Admitted prime guttler and guzzler—O swine!—
To honor thy headship, those tosspots so swilled
That out of their table there sprouted a vine
Whence each claimed a cluster, awaiting thy sign

To out knife, off mouthful: when—who could suppose
Such malice in magic?—each sot woke and found
Cold steel but an inch from the neighbor's red nose
He took for a grape-bunch!

**FUST**
Does that so astound
Sagacity such as ye boast,—who surround

Your mate with eyes staring, hairs standing erect
At his magical feats? Are good burghers unversed
In the humors of toping? Full oft, I suspect,
Ye, counting your fingers, call thumbkin their first,
And reckon a groat every guilder disbursed.

What marvel if wags, while the skinker fast brimmed
Their glass with rare tipple's enticement, should gloat
—Befooled and beflustered—through optics drink-dimmed—
On this draught and that, till each found in his throat
Our Rhenish smack rightly as Raphal? For, note—

They fancied—their fuddling deceived them so grossly—
That liquor sprang out of the table itself
Through gimlet-holes drilled there,—nor noticed how closely
The skinker kept plying my guests, from the shelf
O'er their heads, with the potable madness. No elf

Had need to persuade them a vine rose umbrageous,
Fruit-bearing, thirst-quenching! Enough! I confess
To many such fool-pranks, but none so outrageous

That Satan was called in to help me: excess
I own to, I grieve at—no more and no less.

\*    \*    \*    \*    \*

**SECOND FRIEND**
Strange honors were heaped on thee—medal for breast,
Chain for neck, sword for thigh: not a lord of the land
But acknowledged thee peer! What ambition possessed
A goldsmith by trade, with craft's grime on his hand,
To seek such associates?

**FUST**
Spare taunts! Understand—

I submit me! Of vanities under the sun,
Pride seized me at last as concupiscence first,
Crapulosity ever: true Fiends, every one,
Haled this way and that my poor soul: thus amerced—
Forgive and forget me!

**FIRST FRIEND**
Had flesh sinned the worst,

Yet help were in counsel: the Church could absolve:
But say not men truly thou barredst escape
By signing and sealing ...

**SECOND FRIEND**
On me must devolve
The task of extracting ...

**FIRST FRIEND**
Shall Barnabites ape
Us Dominican experts?

**SEVENTH FRIEND**
Nay, Masters,—agape

When Hell yawns for a soul, 't is myself claim the task
Of extracting, by just one plain question, God's truth!
Where 's Peter Genesheim thy partner? I ask
Why, cloistered up still in thy room, the pale youth
Slaves tongue-tied—thy trade brooks no tattling forsooth!

No less he, thy famulus, suffers entrapping,
Succumbs to good fellowship: barrel a-broach
Runs freely nor needs any subsequent tapping:

Quoth Peter, "That room, none but I dare approach,
Holds secrets will help me to ride in my coach."

He prattles, we profit: in brief, he assures
Thou hast taught him to speak so that all men may hear
—Each alike, wide world over, Jews, Pagans, Turks, Moors,
The same as we Christians—speech heard far and near
At one and the same magic moment!

**FUST**
That 's clear!

Said he—how?

**SEVENTH FRIEND**
Is it like he was licensed to learn?
Who doubts but thou dost this by aid of the Fiend?
Is it so? So it is, for thou smilest! Go, burn
To ashes, since such proves thy portion, unscreened
By bell, book and candle! Yet lately I weened

Balm yet was in Gilead,—some healing in store
For the friend of my bosom. Men said thou wast sunk
In a sudden despondency: not, as before,
Fust gallant and gay with his pottle and punk,
But sober, sad, sick as one yesterday drunk!

\*    \*    \*    \*    \*

**FUST**
Spare Fust, then, thus contrite!—who, youthful and healthy,
Equipped for life's struggle with culture of mind,
Sound flesh and sane soul in coherence, born wealthy,
Nay, wise—how he wasted endowment designed
For the glory of God and the good of mankind!

That much were misused such occasions of grace
Ye well may upbraid him, who bows to the rod.
But this should bid anger to pity give place—
He has turned from the wrong, in the right path to plod,
Makes amends to mankind and craves pardon of God.

"Yea, friends, even now from my lips the Heureka—
Soul saved!" was nigh bursting—unduly elate!
Have I brought Man advantage, or hatched—so to speak—a
Strange serpent, no cygnet? 'T is this I debate
Within me. Forbear, and leave Fust to his fate!

\*    \*    \*    \*    \*

**FIRST FRIEND**
So abject, late lofty? Methinks I spy respite.
Make clean breast, discover what mysteries hide
In thy room there!

**SECOND FRIEND**
Ay, out with them! Do Satan despite!
Remember what caused his undoing was pride!

**FIRST FRIEND**
Dumb devil! Remains one resource to be tried!

\*    \*    \*    \*    \*

**SECOND FRIEND**
Exorcise!

**SEVENTH FRIEND**
Nay, first—is there any remembers
In substance that potent "Ne pulvis"—a psalm
Whereof some live spark haply lurks 'mid the embers
Which choke in my brain. Talk of "Gilead and balm"?
I mind me, sung half through, this gave such a qualm

To Asmodeus inside of a Hussite, that, queasy,
He broke forth in brimstone with curses. I'm strong
In—at least the commencement: the rest should go easy,
Friends helping. "Ne pulvis et ignis" ...

**SIXTH FRIEND**
All wrong!

**FIFTH FRIEND**
I 've conned till I captured the whole.

**SEVENTH FRIEND**
Get along!

"Ne pulvis et cinis superbe te geras,
Nam fulmina" ...

**SIXTH FRIEND**
Fiddlestick! Peace, dolts and dorrs!
Thus runs it "Ne Numinis fulmina feras"—
Then "Hominis perfidi justa sunt sors
Fulmen et grando et horrida mors."

*   *   *   *   *

**SEVENTH FRIEND**
You blunder ... "Irati ne."

**SIXTH FRIEND**
Mind your own business!

**FIFTH FRIEND**
I do not so badly, who gained the monk's leave
To study an hour his choice parchment. A dizziness
May well have surprised me. No Christian dares thieve,
Or I scarce had returned him his treasure. These cleave:

"Nos pulvis et cinis, trementes, gementes,
Venimus"—some such word—"ad te, Domine!
Da lumen, juvamen, ut sancta sequentes
Cor ... corda" ... Plague take it!

**SEVENTH FRIEND**
—"erecta sint spe:"
Right text, ringing rhyme, and ripe Latin for me!

*   *   *   *   *

**SIXTH FRIEND**
A Canon's self wrote it me fair: I was tempted
To part with the sheepskin.

**SEVENTH FRIEND**
Didst grasp and let go
Such a godsend, thou Judas? My purse had been emptied
Ere part with the prize!

**FUST**
Do I dream? Say ye so?
Clouds break, then! Move, world! I have gained my "Pou sto"!

I am saved: Archimedes, salute me!

**OMNES**
Assistance!
Help, Angels! He summons ... Aroint thee!—by name,
His familiar!

**FUST**
Approach!

**OMNES**

Devil, keep thy due distance!

**FUST**

Be tranquillized, townsmen! The knowledge ye claim
Behold, I prepare to impart. Praise or blame,—

Your blessing or banning, whatever betide me,
At last I accept. The slow travail of years,
The long-teeming brain's birth—applaud me, deride me,—
At last claims revealment. Wait!

**SEVENTH FRIEND**

Wait till appears
Uncaged Archimedes cooped-up there?

**SECOND FRIEND**

Who fears?

Here 's have at thee!

**SEVENTH FRIEND**

Correctly now! "Pulvis et cinis" ...

**FUST**

The verse ye so value, it happens I hold
In my memory safe from initium to finis.
Word for word, I produce you the whole, plain enrolled,
Black letters, white paper—no scribe's red and gold!

\*     \*     \*     \*     \*

**OMNES**

Aroint thee!

**FUST**

I go and return.

[He enters the inner room.

**FIRST FRIEND**

Ay, 't is "ibis"
No doubt: but as boldly "redibis"—who 'll say?
I rather conjecture "in Orco peribis!"

**SEVENTH FRIEND**

Come, neighbors!

**SIXTH FRIEND**
I 'm with you! Show courage and stay
Hell's outbreak? Sirs, cowardice here wins the day!

\*    \*    \*    \*    \*

**FIFTH FRIEND**
What luck had that student of Bamberg who ventured
To peep in the cell where a wizard of note
Was busy in getting some black deed debentured
By Satan? In dog's guise there sprang at his throat
A flame-breathing fury. Fust favors, I note,

An ugly huge lurcher!

**SEVENTH FRIEND**
If I placed reliance
As thou, on the beads thou art telling so fast,
I 'd risk just a peep through the keyhole.

**SIXTH FRIEND**
Appliance
Of ear might be safer. Five minutes are past.

**OMNES**
Saints, save us! The door is thrown open at last!

\*    \*    \*    \*    \*

**FUST** [re-enters, the door closing behind him]
As I promised, behold I perform! Apprehend you
The object I offer is poison or pest?
Receive without harm from the hand I extend you
A gift that shall set every scruple at rest!
Shrink back from mere paper-strips? Try them and test!

Still hesitate? Myk,-was it thou who lamentedst
Thy five wits clean failed thee to render aright
A poem read once and no more?—who repentedst
Vile pelf had induced thee to banish from sight
The characters none but our clerics indite?

Take and keep!

**FIRST FRIEND**
Blessed Mary and all Saints about her!

**SECOND FRIEND**
What imps deal so deftly,—five minutes suffice
To play thus the penman?

**THIRD FRIEND**
By Thomas the Doubter,
Five minutes, no more!

**FOURTH FRIEND**
Out on arts that entice
Such scribes to do homage!

**FIFTH FRIEND**
Stay! Once—and now twice—

Yea, a third time, my sharp eye completes the inspection
Of line after line, the whole series, and finds
Each letter join each—not a fault for detection!
Such upstrokes, such downstrokes, such strokes of all kinds
In the criss-cross, all perfect!

**SIXTH FRIEND**
There 's nobody minds

His quill-craft with more of a conscience, o'er-scratches
A sheepskin more nimbly and surely with ink,
Than Paul the Sub-Prior: here 's paper that matches
His parchment with letter on letter, no link
Overleapt—underlost!

**SEVENTH FRIEND**
No erasure, I think—

No blot, I am certain!

**FUST**
Accept the new treasure!

**SIXTH FRIEND**
I remembered full half!

**SEVENTH FRIEND**
But who other than I
(Bear witness, bystanders!) when he broke the measure
Repaired fault with "fulmen"?

**FUST**
Put bickerings by!

Here 's for thee—thee—and thee, too: at need a supply

[Distributing Proofs.

For Mayence, though seventy times seven should muster!
How now? All so feeble of faith that no face
Which fronts me but whitens—or yellows, were juster?
Speak out lest I summon my Spirits!

**OMNES**
Grace—grace!
Call none of thy—helpmates! We 'll answer apace!

My paper—and mine—and mine also—they vary
In nowise—agree in each tittle and jot!
Fust, how—why was this?

**FUST**
Shall such "Cur" miss a "quare"?
Within, there! Throw doors wide! Behold who complot
To abolish the scribe's work—blur, blunder and blot!

[The doors open, and the Press is discovered in operation.

Brave full-bodied birth of this brain that conceived thee
In splendor and music,—sustained the slow drag
Of the days stretched to years dim with doubt,—yet believed thee,
Had faith in thy first leap of life! Pulse might flag—
—Mine fluttered how faintly!—Arch-moment might lag

Its longest—I bided, made light of endurance,
Held hard by the hope of an advent which—dreamed,
Is done now: night yields to the dawn's reassurance:
I have thee—I hold thee—my fancy that seemed,
My fact that proves palpable! Ay, Sirs, I schemed

Completion that 's fact: see this Engine—be witness
Yourselves of its working! Nay, handle my Types!
Each block bears a Letter: in order and fitness
I range them. Turn, Peter, the winch! See, it gripes
What 's under! Let loose—? draw! In regular stripes

Lies plain, at one pressure, your poem—touched, tinted,
Turned out to perfection! The sheet, late a blank,
Filled—ready for reading,—not written but PRINTED!
Omniscient omnipotent God, thee I thank,
Thee ever, thee only!—thy creature that shrank

From no task thou, Creator, imposedst! Creation
Revealed me no object, from insect to Man,
But bore thy hand's impress: earth glowed with salvation:
"Hast sinned? Be thou saved, Fust! Continue my plan,
Who spake and earth was: with my word things began.

"As sound so went forth, to the sight be extended
Word's mission henceforward! The task I assign,
Embrace—thy allegiance to evil is ended!
Have cheer, soul impregnate with purpose! Combine
Soul and body, give birth to my concept—called thine!

"Far and wide, North and South, East and West, have dominion
O'er thought, wingèd wonder, O Word! Traverse world
In sun-flash and sphere-song! Each beat of thy pinion
Bursts night, beckons day: once Truth's banner unfurled,
Where 's Falsehood? Sun-smitten, to nothingness hurled!"

More humbly—so, friends, did my fault find redemption.
I sinned, soul-entoiled by the tether of sense:
My captor reigned master: I plead no exemption,
From Satan's award to his servant: defence
From the fiery and final assault would be—whence?

By making—as man might—to truth restitution!
Truth is God: trample lies and lies' father, God's foe!
Fix fact fast: truths change by an hour's revolution:
What deed's very doer, unaided, can show
How 't was done a year—month—week—day—minute ago?

At best, he relates it—another reports it—
A third—nay, a thousandth records it: and still
Narration, tradition, no step but distorts it,
As down from truth's height it goes sliding until
At the low level lie-mark it stops—whence no skill

Of the scribe, intervening too tardily, rescues
—Once fallen—lost fact from lie's fate there. What scribe
—Eyes horny with poring, hands crippled with desk-use,
Brains fretted by fancies—the volatile tribe
That tease weary watchers—can boast that no bribe

Shuts eye and frees hand and remits brain from toiling?
Truth gained—can we stay, at whatever the stage,
Truth a-slide,—save her snow from its ultimate soiling
In mire,—by some process, stamp promptly on page
Fact spoiled by pen's plodding, make truth heritage

Not merely of clerics, but poured out, full measure,
On clowns—every mortal endowed with a mind?
Read, gentle and simple! Let labor win leisure
At last to bid truth do all duty assigned,
Not pause at the noble but pass to the hind!

How bring to effect such swift sure simultaneous
Unlimited multiplication? How spread
By an arm-sweep a hand-throw—no helping extraneous—
Truth broadcast o'er Europe? "The goldsmith," I said,
"Graves limning on gold: why not letters on lead?"

So, Tuscan artificer, grudge not thy pardon
To me who played false, made a furtive descent,
Found the sly secret workshop,—thy genius kept guard on
Too slackly for once,—and surprised thee low-bent
O'er thy labor—some chalice thy tool would indent

With a certain free scroll-work framed round by a border
Of foliage and fruitage: no scratching so fine,
No shading so shy but, in ordered disorder,
Each flourish came clear,—unbewildered by shine,
On the gold, irretrievably right, lay each line.

How judge if thy hand worked thy will? By reviewing,
Revising again and again, piece by piece,
Tool's performance,—this way, as I watched. 'T was through glueing
A paper-like film-stuff—thin, smooth, void of crease,
On each cut of the graver: press hard! at release,

No mark on the plate but the paper showed double:
His work might proceed: as he judged—space or speck
Up he filled, forth he flung—was relieved thus from trouble
Lest wrong—once—were right never more: what could check
Advancement, completion? Thus lay at my beck—

At my call—triumph likewise! "For," cried I, "what hinders
That graving turns Printing? Stamp one word—not one
But fifty such, phœnix-like, spring from death's cinders,—
Since death is word's doom, clerics hide from the sun
As some churl closets up this rare chalice." Go, run

Thy race now, Fust's child! High, O Printing, and holy
Thy mission! These types, see, I chop and I change
Till the words, every letter, a pageful, not slowly
Yet surely lies fixed: last of all, I arrange
A paper beneath, stamp it, loosen it!

**FIRST FRIEND**
Strange!

\*   \*   \*   \*   \*

**SECOND FRIEND**
How simple exceedingly!

**FUST**
Bustle, my Schœffer!
Set type,—quick, Genesheim! Turn screw now!

**THIRD FRIEND**
Just that!

**FOURTH FRIEND**
And no such vast miracle!

**FUST**
"Plough with my heifer,
Ye find out my riddle," quoth Samson, and pat
He speaks to the purpose. Grapes squeezed in the vat

Yield to sight and to taste what is simple—a liquid
Mere urchins may sip: but give time, let ferment—
You 've wine, manhood's master! Well, "rectius si quid
Novistis im-per-ti-te!" Wait the event,
Then weigh the result! But, whate'er Thy intent,

O Thou, the one force in the whole variation
Of visible nature,—at work—do I doubt?—
From Thy first to our last, in perpetual creation—
A film hides us from Thee—'twixt inside and out,
A film, on this earth where Thou bringest about

New marvels, new forms of the glorious, the gracious,
We bow to, we bless for: no star bursts heaven's dome
But Thy finger impels it, no weed peeps audacious
Earth's clay-floor from out, but Thy finger makes room
For one world's-want the more in Thy Cosmos: presume

Shall Man, Microcosmos, to claim the conception
Of grandeur, of beauty, in thought, word or deed?
I toiled, but Thy light on my dubiousest step shone:
If I reach the glad goal, is it I who succeed
Who stumbled at starting tripped up by a reed,

Or Thou? Knowledge only and absolute, glory

As utter be Thine who concedest a spark
Of Thy spheric perfection to earth's transitory
Existences! Nothing that lives, but Thy mark
Gives law to—life's light: what is doomed to the dark?

Where 's ignorance? Answer, creation! What height,
What depth has escaped Thy commandment —to Know?
What birth in the ore-bed but answers aright
Thy sting at its heart which impels—bids "E'en so,
Not otherwise more or be motionless,—grow,

"Decline, disappear!" Is the plant in default
How to bud, when to branch forth? The bird and the beast
—Do they doubt if their safety be found in assault
Or escape? Worm or fly, of what atoms the least
But follows light's guidance,—will famish, not feast?

In such various degree, fly and worm, ore and plant,
All know, none is witless: around each, a wall
Encloses the portion, or ample or scant,
Of Knowledge: beyond which one hair's breadth, for all
Lies blank—not so much as a blackness—a pall

Some sense unimagined must penetrate: plain
Is only old license to stand, walk or sit,
Move so far and so wide in the narrow domain
Allotted each nature for life's use: past it
How immensity spreads does he guess? Not a whit.

Does he care? Just as little. Without? No, within
Concerns him? he Knows. Man Ignores—thanks to Thee
Who madest him know, but—in knowing—begin
To know still new vastness of knowledge must be
Outside him—to enter, to traverse, in fee

Have and hold! "Oh, Man's ignorance!" hear the fool whine!
How were it, for better or worse, didst thou grunt
Contented with sapience—the lot of the swine
Who knows he was born for just truffles to hunt?—
Monks' Paradise—"Semper sint res uti sunt!"

No, Man's the prerogative—knowledge once gained—
To ignore,—find new knowledge to press for, to swerve
In pursuit of, no, not for a moment: attained—
Why, onward through ignorance! Dare and deserve!
As still to its asymptote speedeth the curve,

So approximates Man—Thee, who, reachable not,

Hast formed him to yearningly follow Thy whole
Sole and single omniscience!
Such, friends, is my lot:
I am back with the world: one more step to the goal
Thanks for reaching I render—Fust's help to Man's soul!

Mere mechanical help? So the hand gives a toss
To the falcon,—aloft once, spread pinions and fly,
Beat air far and wide, up and down and across!
My Press strains a-tremhle: whose masterful eye
Will be first, in new regions, new truth to descry?

Give chase, soul! Be sure each new capture consigned
To my Types will go forth to the world, like God's bread
—Miraculous food not for body but mind,
Truth's manna! How say you? Put case that, instead
Of old leasing and lies, we superiorly fed

These Heretics, Hussites ...

**FIRST FRIEND**
First answer my query!
If saved, art thou happy?

**FUST**
I was and I am.

**FIRST FRIEND**
Thy visage confirms it: how comes, then, that—weary
And woe-begone late—was it show, was it sham?—
We found thee sunk thiswise?

**SECOND FRIEND**
—In need of the dram

From the flask which a provident neighbor might carry!

**FUST**
Ah, friends, the fresh triumph soon flickers, fast fades!
I hailed Word's dispersion: could heartleaps but tarry!
Through me does Print furnish Truth wings? The same aids
Cause Falsehood to range just as widely. What raids

On a region undreamed of does Printing enable
Truth's foe to effect! Printed leasing and lies
May speed to the world's farthest corner— gross fable
No less than pure fact—to impede, neutralize,
Abolish God's gift and Man's gain!

**FIRST FRIEND**
Dost surmise

What struck me at first blush? Our Beghards, Waldenses,
Jeronimites, Hussites—does one show his head,
Spout heresy now? Not a priest in his senses
Deigns answer mere speech, but piles fagots instead,
Refines as by fire, and, him silenced, all 's said.

Whereas if in future I pen an opuscule
Defying retort, as of old when rash tongues
Were easy to tame,—straight some knave of the Huss-School
Prints answer forsooth! Stop invisible lungs?
The barrel of blasphemy broached once, who bungs?

\*   \*   \*   \*   \*

**SECOND FRIEND**
Does my sermon, next Easter, meet fitting acceptance?
Each captious disputative boy has his quirk
"An cuique credendum sit?" Well, the Church kept "ans"
In order till Fust set his engine at work!
What trash will come flying from Jew, Moor, and Turk

When, goosequill, thy reign o'er the world is abolished!
Goose—ominous name! With a goose woe began:
Quoth Huss—which means "goose" in his idiom unpolished—
"Ye burn now a Goose: there succeeds me a Swan
Ye shall find quench your fire!"

**FUST**
I foresee such a man.

Robert Browning – A Short Biography

He is the equal of any Victorian Poet that could be mentioned. However, Browning continues to be in the shadow of Tennyson, Arnold, Hopkins, Morris and many others.

Robert Browning was born on May 7th, 1812 in Walworth in the parish of Camberwell, London. He was baptized on June 14th, 1812, at Lock's Fields Independent Chapel, York Street, Walworth.

Browning's early years were certainly very interesting. His mother was an excellent pianist and a very devout evangelical Christian. His father, who worked as a clerk at the Bank of England, was also an artist, scholar, antiquarian, and collector of books and pictures. Indeed, he amassed more than 6,000 volumes of rare books including works in Greek, Hebrew, Latin, French, Italian, and Spanish. For the young and curious Browning, it was a wonderful resource, added to which his father was a guiding force in his education.

Many accounts attest that Browning was already proficient at reading and writing by the age of five. He is said to have been a bright but anxious student and to have studied and learnt Latin, Greek, and French by the time he was fourteen. From fourteen to sixteen he was educated at home, tutored in music, drawing, dancing, and horsemanship. Certainly, language and the arts were two areas the young Browning both absorbed and pushed himself towards.

At the age of twelve he wrote a volume of Byronic verse he called Incondita, which his parents attempted to have published. The attempts were unsuccessful and, disappointed, Browning destroyed the work.

In 1825, a cousin gave Browning a collection of Percy Bysshe Shelley's poetry; Browning was so enamored with the poems that he asked for the rest of Shelley's works for his thirteenth birthday. In fact, Browning then went the extra mile, declaring himself to be both a vegetarian and an atheist in honour of his hero.

Intriguingly it seems that the rejection of his first volume didn't dim his appreciation of other poets, but it appears to have stopped him writing any poems between the ages of thirteen and twenty.

In 1828, Browning enrolled at the newly-opened University of London. He was uncomfortable with the experience and he soon left, anxious to read and absorb at his own pace.

His education which, overall is notably rambling and lacks a structure that many of his artistic contemporaries enjoyed, i.e. excellent public schooling and then a degree at Oxford or Cambridge, may present many of his critics with ammunition to criticize, but alternatively his hap-hazard education certainly contributed to many of the references that baffled both critics and his audience, but they tellingly show the breath and scale of what he could turn words too. What others would call obscure references were, to Browning, remarkably obvious.

Browning's early career was very promising. His long poem Pauline (of which only a fragment was ever finished and published) brought him to the attention of the Pre-Raphaelite master Dante Gabriel Rossetti and his difficult Paracelsus (published in 1835) was warmly admired by both Dickens and Wordsworth.

In the 1830s he met the actor William Macready and was encouraged to develop and turn his talents to the stage by writing verse drama. But these plays, including Strafford, which ran for five nights in 1837, and those contained within the Bells and Pomegranates series, were, for the most part, unsuccessful.

During this period Browning began to discover that his real talents lay in taking a single character and allowing that character to discover more about himself by revealing further personal aspects of himself in his speeches; the dramatic monologue. The techniques he developed through this—especially the use of diction, rhythm, and symbol—are regarded as his most important contribution to poetry. They would later influence such major poets of the 20th Century as Ezra Pound, T. S. Eliot, and Robert Frost.

By 1840, with the publication of Sordello, the tide turned somewhat. Many thought he was being deliberately obscure, opaque beyond measure and his poetry for the next decade or so was not eagerly acquired or talked about.

As Browning attempted to rehabilitate his career he began a relationship with Elizabeth Barrett in 1845. He had read her poems and, being totally charmed by their quality, was determined to meet her. The poetess was better known than the younger Browning but suffered from a debilitating illness and was also subject to the harsh behaviour of her over-bearing father. Nevertheless, the new couple were soon inseparable.

Her father, as he did with any of his children that married, disinherited her. Despite this she had some money from her own resources and sensing that the best outcome for both the relationship and her own health was to move abroad the couple did just that. After a private marriage at St Marylebone Parish Church, in September 1846, they journeyed to Europe to honeymoon in Paris.

Their new life now took them to Italy, first to Pisa and a little later to Florence. There they absorbed life and one another.

But in the short term the literary assault on Browning's work did not let up. He was now criticized by such patrician writers as Charles Kingsley for his abandonment of England for foreign lands. Browning could do little to answer these attacks except to compose with his pen and continue with his poetical journey.

The Browning's were well respected, and even famous. Elizabeth health began to improve, she grew stronger and in 1849, at the age of 43, between four miscarriages, she gave birth to a son, Robert Wiedeman Barrett Browning, whom they nicknamed "Penini" or "Pen",

Intriguingly despite his growing reputation and return to form as a poet he was more often than not known as 'Elizabeth Barrett's husband'.

Work flowed from his pen that was to ensure his reputation as one of England's leading poets. When his collection Men and Women was published in 1855 it contained some of his finest lines. It was dedicated to Elizabeth. Life had begun to smile handsome rewards upon the Brownings.

Victorian society was very much taken with all things spiritualist. It was not enough to have command of much of the globe through Empire, they wished to know and explore wherever they could. The spirit world beckoned their interest. Browning dissented from this view believing it was all a hoax and a fraud. Elizabeth, however, was inclined to believe and this caused several disagreements between the couple.

They attended a séance by Daniel Dunglas Home, in July 1855. (Home was a famous and clamored after Scottish physical medium with the reported ability to levitate and speak with the dead). It is said that during this séance a spirit face materialised. Home then claimed it was the face of Browning's son who had died in infancy. Browning seized the 'materialisation' which turned out to be Home's bare foot. Browning had never lost a son in infancy.

After the séance, Browning wrote an angry letter to The Times, in which he said: "the whole display of hands, spirit utterances etc., was a cheat and imposture."

The Browning's time in Italy were immensely rewarding years for both their personal and professional lives. Browning encouraged her to include Sonnets from the Portuguese in her published works, these beautiful poems are undoubtedly one of the highlights of English love poetry.

Elizabeth had become quite politicised during these years. Engrossed in Italian politics (which was continuing to slowly re-unify the country), she issued a small volume of political poems entitled Poems before Congress (1860) most of which were written to express her sympathy with the Italian cause after the earlier outbreak of The Second Italian Independence War in 1859. In England they caused uproar. Conservative magazines such as Blackwood's and the Saturday Review labelled her a fanatic. She dedicated the book to her husband.

But in 1861 tragedy struck.

The couple had spent the winter of 1860–61 in Rome when Elizabeth's health deteriorated again and they returned to Florence in early June. However, these turned out to be her final weeks. Only morphine would now still the pain. She died in Browning's arms on June 29th, 1861. Browning said that she died "smilingly, happily, and with a face like a girl's .... Her last word was .... "Beautiful".

Her burial took place in the nearby Protestant English Cemetery of Florence. The local people were deeply saddened, and shops closed their doors in grief and respect.

Browning and their son were obviously devastated. Unable to bear being in Florence without Elizabeth they soon returned to London to live at 19 Warwick Crescent, Maida Vale.

As he re-integrated himself back into the London literary scene he began to finally receive the proper praise, respect and reputation that his works deserved.

Browning went on to publish Dramatis Personæ (1864), and The Ring and the Book (1868–1869). The latter, based on an "old yellow book" which told of a seventeenth-century Italian murder trial, received wide and generous critical acclaim. Although by now he was in the twilight of a long and prolific career, that had achieved some notable ups and downs, he was respected and indeed renowned for his talents and works.

In 1878, he revisited Italy for the first time since Elizabeth's death. He would return there on several further occasions but never to Florence.

Such was the esteem he was held in that The Browning Society was founded in 1881. Although he had never obtained a degree (something that set him apart from many other Victorian poets) he was now awarded honorary degrees from Oxford University in 1882 and then the University of Edinburgh in 1884.

In 1887, Browning produced the major work of his later years, Parleyings with Certain People of Importance in Their Day. Browning now spoke with his own voice as he engaged in a series of dialogues with long-forgotten figures of literary, artistic, and philosophic history. Unfortunately, both the critics and public were completely baffled by this.

On April 7th, 1889 Browning attended a dinner party at the home of his friend, the artist Rudolf Lehmann. The highlight of which was a recording made on a wax cylinder on an Edison cylinder phonograph. On the recording, which still exists, Browning recites part of How They Brought the Good News from Ghent to Aix, and can even be heard apologising when he forgets the words.

The recording was first played in 1890 on the anniversary of his death, at a gathering of his admirers, it was said to be the first time anyone's voice 'had been heard from beyond the grave'.

His last work Asolando: Fancies and Facts (1889), returned to his brief and concise lyric verse that was so popular.  It was published on the day of his death on December 12th, 1889, Robert Browning was at his son's home Ca' Rezzonico in Venice.

He was buried in Poets' Corner in Westminster Abbey; his grave lies immediately adjacent to that of Alfred Tennyson.

Among the many who have publicly acknowledged their literary debt to him are Henry James, Oscar Wilde, George Bernard Shaw, G. K. Chesterton, Ezra Pound, Jorge Luis Borges, and Vladimir Nabokov.


Robert Browning - A Concise Bibliography

*Here follows a list of the plays and poetry volumes published during his lifetime. Poems of particular worth are noted from within those volumes.*

Pauline: A Fragment of a Confession (1833)
Paracelsus (1835)
Strafford (play) (1837)
Sordello (1840)
Bells and Pomegranates No. I: Pippa Passes (play) (1841)
      *The Year's at the Spring*
Bells and Pomegranates No. II: King Victor and King Charles (play) (1842)
Bells and Pomegranates No. III: Dramatic Lyrics (1842)
      *Porphyria's Lover*
      *Soliloquy of the Spanish Cloister*
      *My Last Duchess*
      *The Pied Piper of Hamelin*
      *Count Gismond*
      *Johannes Agricola in Meditation*
Bells and Pomegranates No. IV: The Return of the Druses (play) (1843)
Bells and Pomegranates No. V: A Blot in the 'Scutcheon (play) (1843)
Bells and Pomegranates No. VI: Colombe's Birthday (play) (1844)
Bells and Pomegranates No. VII: Dramatic Romances and Lyrics (1845)
      *The Laboratory*
      *How They Brought the Good News from Ghent to Aix*
      *The Bishop Orders His Tomb at Saint Praxed's Church*
      *The Lost Leader*
      *Home Thoughts from Abroad*
      *Meeting at Night*
Bells and Pomegranates No. VIII: Luria and A Soul's Tragedy (plays) (1846)

Christmas-Eve and Easter-Day (1850)
An Essay on Percy Bysshe Shelley (essay) (1852)
Two Poems (1854)
Men and Women (1855)
  *Love Among the Ruins*
  *A Toccata of Galuppi's*
  *Childe Roland to the Dark Tower Came*
  *Fra Lippo Lippi*
  *Andrea Del Sarto*
  *The Patriot*
  *The Last Ride Together*
  *Memorabilia*
  *Cleon*
  *How It Strikes a Contemporary*
  *The Statue and the Bust*
  *A Grammarian's Funeral*
  *An Epistle Containing the Strange Medical Experience of Karshish, the Arab Physician*
  *Bishop Blougram's Apology*
  *Master Hugues of Saxe-Gotha*
  *By the Fire-side*
Dramatis Personae (1864)
  *Caliban upon Setebos*
  *Rabbi Ben Ezra*
  *Abt Vogler*
  *Mr. Sludge, "The Medium"*
  *Prospice*
  *A Death in the Desert*
The Ring and the Book (1868–69)
Balaustion's Adventure (1871)
Prince Hohenstiel-Schwangau, Saviour of Society (1871)
Fifine at the Fair (1872)
Red Cotton Night-Cap Country, or, Turf and Towers (1873)
Aristophanes' Apology (1875)
  *Thamuris Marching*
The Inn Album (1875)
Pacchiarotto, and How He Worked in Distemper (1876)
  *Numpholeptos*
The Agamemnon of Aeschylus (1877)
La Saisiaz and The Two Poets of Croisic (1878)
Dramatic Idylls (1879)
Dramatic Idylls: Second Series (1880)
  *Pan and Luna*
Jocoseria (1883)
Ferishtah's Fancies (1884)
Parleyings with Certain People of Importance in Their Day (1887)
Asolando (1889)
  *Prologue*
  *Summum Bonum*

*Bad Dreams III*
*Flute-Music, with an Accompaniment*
*Epilogue*

www.ingramcontent.com/pod-product-compliance
Lightning Source LLC
Chambersburg PA
CBHW060129050426
42448CB00010B/2038